Georgios I. Doukidis / Ec

Developing Expert Systems

Chartwell-Bratt

Studentlitteratur

Chartwell-Bratt (Publishing and Training) Ltd
ISBN 0-86238-196-7

Index prepared by Indexing Specialists Ltd, Hove, East Sussex, UK

Printed in Sweden,
Studentlitteratur, Lund

ISBN 91-44-29021-7 1 2 3 4 5 6 7 8 9 10 | 1992 91 90 89 88

To

"Giagia" Rodopi
"Oma" Heymons

Trademarks

Apple is a registered trademark of Apple Computers Inc.
ART is a trademark of Inference Corp.
CATS-1 is a trademark of General Electric Crop.
dBASE II and dBASE III are registered trademarks of Ashton-Tate.
Dipmeter Advisor is a trademark of Schlumberger-Doll Research.
Expert-Ease is a copyright product of Intelligent Terminals Ltd.
Explorer is a trademark of Texas Instruments Inc.
IBM is a registered trademark of International Business Machines, Inc.
Insight 2+ is a trademark of Level Five Research, Inc.
KEE is a trademark of Intellicorp.
Knowledge Craft is a trademark of Carnegie Group, Inc.
Lotus and 1-2-3 are registered trademarks of Lotus Development.
Macintosh is a trademark licensed to Apple Computers Inc.
muLISP is a trademark of Soft Warehouse Inc.
MS-DOS is a trademark of MicroSoft Corporation.
OPS5 is a trademark of Verac Inc.
Turbo Pascal is a registered trademark of Borland International, Inc.
Xi+ and Xi Rule are trademarks of Expertech Ltd.
XCON is a trademark of Digital Equipment Corporation.

PESYS and ASPES are available from the authors. For details about these systems please contact the authors at:

Dr G I Doukidis & Mr E A Whitley
Department of Information Systems
London School of Economics and Political Science
Houghton Street
London WC2A 2AE

Preface

Expert systems are amongst the most talked about computer programs to develop in recent years. Some see them as a means of automating knowledge based work in the same way that the steam engine automated manual work in the (first) industrial revolution, offering the possibility for huge cost savings and profits. Others hold that the programs are dangerous concepts, thought to be more powerful than they actually are and a poor model of the human expertise they aim to automate.

For the executive who is investigating the possibility of using expert systems within a company, the book provides a general introduction to the domain. Whilst many other books simply extol the virtues of expert system technology we hope to provide a more balanced view by pointing out the limitations of and problems with expert systems.

By explaining how simple expert systems work, we provide the reader with a firm understanding of the terminology and techniques involved in the field so that the advertising hype can be separated from the useful features of available expert systems.

The development of an expert system involves a number of steps. Firstly the knowledge of the expert must be elicited. Once this knowledge has been elicited it must be formalised and tested. The formalised knowledge is then converted into a computerised form and is added to the Expert System. The combination of expert system, with its explanation facilities etc., and knowledge base must then be tested in the real world. Further modifications to the system are then made until it is suitable for final release.

The book was partially based on a course taught to Msc Students in the Analysis, Design and Management of Information Systems at the London School of Economics and Political Science and, despite its origins, it is a suitable textbook for use at all levels of teaching. In contrast to many other texts the book covers all aspects of developing expert systems, not only the writing of the knowledge bases used in the system.

For more advanced research it also describes a number of theoretical points that have been developed in work at the London School of Economics.

The book is divided into two parts - theory and practice. The first four chapters cover the "theoretical" background to the subject, whilst chapters six to ten cover expert systems development on a practical basis. This is done in two ways, the first is through the use of an Expert System Shell, the second is by using an AI symbolic programming language.

Much of the work is based on current research being undertaken at the school, in particular chapter five is based on the paper "A knowledge acquisition case study: towards an intergrated approach of knowledge elicitation techniques" by Poulymenakou and Doukidis. The PESYS system, developed by the authors and described in chapters six, seven and eight is a development of a system described in the paper "Developing and running Expert Systems with PESYS". References for both these papers can be found in the bibliography.

Chapter one introduces the domain of Expert Systems and relates it to its background in the field of artificial intelligence. It lists some of the features found in current systems and then examines the market for expert system products.

Chapter two introduces knowledge engineering. The process of knowledge engineering is closely related to the feasibility of the expert system project. If the knowledge of the expert cannot be obtained, the project will not succeed. A number of different techniques are described in detail and some possible methods for testing the knowledge are discussed.

Chapter three is concerned with the representation of knowledge. It mentions the conflicting aims of understandable and computable forms of representation and explains a number of different representations that are currently being used.

Chapter four concerns the different tools that are available to develop expert systems. The relationship with software engineering is also discussed and the possible future requirements for tools are analysed.

Chapter five, the first of the practical applications, is a case study in knowledge acquisition. It demonstrates the processes involved in actual problems and the limitations of theories.

Chapter six introduces the PESYS system and overviews the two phases of the system's use - development and consultation.

Chapter seven gives further details about PESYS, including details about the powerful features that are incorporated into the PESYS rule format.

Chapter eight is made up of two knowledge bases that have been written in PESYS. They demonstrate the power and flexibility of the system.

Chapter nine gives an introduction to the LISP programming language so that the reader can understand the simple Expert System, written in LISP, that is given in the next chapter.

Chapter ten gives a full explanation of the Lisp expert system, detailing the different functions and knowledge structures.

The writing of this book would not have been accomplished without the assistance of a number of colleagues. In particular, Angeliki Poulymenakou who was involved in the case study given in chapter five, Achal Kapila who developed the "How's that!" knowledge base covered in chapter eight and Marios Angelides and Vijal Shah who were involved in the development of the Lisp expert system described in chapter ten. We also appreciate the comments from staff and graduate students in the Information Systems department (who although they may not all be "fans" of expert systems offered useful advice and suggestions). Finally, we must thank the students on the MSC Analysis, Design and Management of Information Systems course at the school whose feedback on the teaching material was very much appreciated.

Edgar A. Whitley and Georgios I. Doukidis

Information Systems
London School of Economics and Political Science
May 1988.

Contents

List of figures

Chapter 1

Introduction to Expert Systems

1.1 Artificial Intelligence

Those cognitive abilities found in human beings that are apparently not found in other living creatures have long proved to be a source of wonder to humans. Attempts to understand these abilities have formed a large basis of what has now become known as science. The "physical" sciences of biology, chemistry and to a lesser extent physics have been involved in discovering how the brain implements, updates and stores these abilities. The social sciences of psychology, linguistics and sociology etc. have, at various degrees of abstraction, tried to understand how these cognitive abilities show themselves in actual behaviour.

Until 1950, when Alan Turing published his seminal paper "Computing machinery and intelligence" (Turing, 1950) the main aim of the sciences was to catalogue and theorise about these abilities in humans. After Turing's paper, philosophically at least, the domain of study was broadened to include the possibility of transferring human "intelligence" onto a machine.

The newly "invented" computers which were already being used to replace the monotonous, labour intensive jobs such as payroll were seen to be the ideal tools to experiment with the notion of automated intelligence. Within a few years experimental systems that could play games of chess, prove theorems in logic and geometry were invented. Whilst these systems were, in general, working on small, so called "toy", domains, they demonstrated that the possibility of making machines "appear more intelligent" was at least a valid area for research.

We use the phrase "appear more intelligent" because there is, at the present time, no acceptable definition of intelligence. The closest one comes to a definition is a list of features that are usually present if an activity appears "intelligent". These features include - the ability to reason, to infer, to prove, to explain as well as to acquire knowledge, the ability to apply knowledge, the ability to teach and to understand natural language.

1.1.1 Definitions of A.I.

The first step in understanding a field is usually to define the subject or frame of reference to be investigated. In many subjects that have not reached a stable maturity (fields in which there are many paradigm shifts in the language of Kuhn (Kuhn, 1962)) there are often conflicting definitions of the field. This is particularly hampered by the fact that problems in A.I. are no longer called A.I. problems once they have been solved. For example, computerised game playing was originally an active field of A.I. research, but Chess programs are no longer considered as A.I. programs. In view of these problems the best we can do is offer a number of different definitions.

A.I. is the science of making machines do things that would require intelligence if done by men. (Minsky, 1968)

Broadly considered, A.I. can be viewed from two standpoints. The first is the scientific standpoint aiming at understanding the mechanisms of human intelligence, the computer being used to provide a simulation to verify theories about intelligence. The second standpoint is the engineering one, whose object is to endow a computer with the intellectual capabilities of people. Most researchers adopt the second standpoint, aiming to make the capabilities of computers approach those of human intelligence without trying to imitate exactly the information processing steps of human beings. (Shirai & Tsujii, 1982)

A.I. is the discipline that aims to understand the nature of human intelligence through the construction of computer programs that imitate intelligent behaviour. (Bonnet, 1985)

A.I. is the study of mental faculties through the use of computational models. (Charniak & McDermott, 1985)

A.I. is the study of how to make computers do things which, at the moment, people are better. (Rich, 1983)

The overall consensus achieved is that A.I. is concerned with automating those human activities that have not been automated before.

1.1.2 Current A.I. Research

At the present time A.I. research can be subdivided into three major areas : Language communication, Environmental manipulation and Knowledge manipulation.

Language communication is concerned with all aspects of linguistics - natural language understanding, whereby a computer "understands" sentences in a natural language such as English, language translation from one natural language into another and speech recognition and generation which involves converting sound patterns into words and back again.

Environmental manipulation is primarily concerned with robots. In particular attention is focused on vision systems - so that the robot can examine objects and places - and tactile techniques so that the robots can manipulate the environment in which they find themselves.

The final major area of A.I. research is that of knowledge manipulation. The general term for the systems in this area is Intelligent Knowledge Based Systems (IKBS). IKBS can be thought of as applied A.I. since in many cases they are used in "real" areas where knowledge, rather than data, is being used.

1.2 Introduction to Expert Systems

As modern industrialised society becomes more specialised the need to have "expert advice" increases rapidly. This necessity is visible in all forms of life - a consumer wishing to buy a new washing machine, for example, needs to base his decision on a wide variety of technical and aesthetic factors before making his choice. In most cases he will ask a sales assistant for "expert advice" in making these decisions. Whilst there is obviously a bias amongst sales staff in favour of the more expensive models, there is also a large amount of "expert knowledge" that will be imparted.

On an industrial level many of the machines in modern factories require "expert advice" if they need to be repaired. Finally management and government teams rely heavily on "expert advice" to help them to plan and implement future policies.

At the present time most of this "expert advice" is provided by humans. Storing expertise in humans, just as having humans doing certain physical tasks, has both advantages and disadvantages. On the positive side humans have initiative and intelligence, they can adapt to new surroundings automatically and make decisions based on new data rapidly. Humans also, however, become ill, move to different jobs, get tired, make irrational decisions, become preoccupied with other matters, die, take a long time to learn things and can only perform one complex task at a time.

The traditional solution to these problems has been to encode this knowledge in manuals and guidebooks. So, for example, one would have a manual for performing task A, a manual for task B etc. If an unusual problem C, then arose, it would be possible to find the solution in a guidebook or by asking the expert directly. The use of manuals and guidebooks is often laborious and expensive and the books take up valuable storage space, so for some of the reasons mentioned above many firms have attempted to use the technique of Expert Systems to store the knowledge of an expert (or group of experts) about a particular problem area in a computable form and then use this stored information if a problem arises.

There are a number of reasons for doing this - firstly the knowledge of an expert who is going to retire soon can be stored so that his knowledge is not lost to the company forever. This can also apply if there is a strong possibility of experts changing jobs, particularly if they take a long time to train. A second reason for implementing expert systems is to lighten the load on the specialists - if an expert system can be created to solve the easier problems in a particular domain then the specialist will be left with the more demanding and rewarding problems to solve.

1.2.1 Expert System definitions

Just as there is a wide divergence of views as to what defines A.I., there are similar problems involved in defining Expert Systems. We now list some definitions:

Expert Systems are programs which perform tasks which are usually performed by experts; they embody expert knowledge and the ability to use that knowledge to solve problems. These programs are restricted in the types of tasks they can perform, but in approaching suitable problems they demonstrate expertise. Knowledge is encoded within such programs, and therefore they are powerful tools. (Hart, 1986)

An Expert System is one that

- handles real-world complex problems requiring an expert's interpretation

- solves these problems using a computer based model of expert human reasoning, reaching the same conclusions that the human expert would reach if faced with a comparable problem.

... A computer based expert system seeks to capture enough of the human specialists knowledge so that it too will solve problems expertly. (Weiss & Kulikowski, 1984)

An expert system is a knowledge based system that emulates expert thought to solve significant problems in a particular domain of expertise. (Sell, 1985)

An expert system is a knowledge based system that emulates expert thought to solve significant problems in a particular domain of expertise. (Jackson, 1986)

An expert system is an intelligent computer program that uses knowledge and inference procedures to solve problems that are difficult enough to require significant human expertise for their solutions. Knowledge necessary to perform at such a level, plus the inference procedures used, can be thought of as a model of the expertise of the best practitioners of the field. (Feigenbaum, 1982)

An expert system is regarded as the embodiment within a computer of a knowledge based component, from an expert skill, in such a form that the system can offer intelligent advice or take an intelligent decision about a processing function. A desirable additional characteristic, which many would consider fundamental, is the capability of the system, on demand, to justify its own line of reasoning in a manner directly intelligible to the enquirer. The style adopted to attain these characteristics is rule-based programming. (British Computer Society)

Most definitions of Expert Systems (including those listed above) can be divided into those that state *what* an expert system does and those that specify *how* it does it.

It is necessary to be very wary with *what* definitions particularly those that state that "an expert system is a computer program that performs the task of a human expert". Payroll clerks are "experts" in the field of paying employees according to various tax and benefit regulations, yet one would not normally call a payroll package an expert system. One attempt at a solution to this problem is to state that Expert Systems are used in areas where an expert's knowledge is not explicitly stated - yet much of the work done by systems analysts is to elicit and formalise these unstated procedures etc.

The definition we favour combines what an expert system does with how it does it as well as showing the differences between it and a standard computer program.

An expert system is a computer program that assists a user by providing information about a particular domain. It does this by manipulating information about the field that has been provided by a number of "experts" in the field. Another important feature of an expert system is that it has the facility to explain/justify the methods it used to provide the information.

1.2.2. Expert System features

We have already described some of the "problems" with human experts; we now list some of the features that successful expert system implementations ought to incorporate: Significant performance capabilities, reasonable response time, a modifiable knowledge base, a suitable user interface and the software should be manufactured using software engineering techniques.

Significant performance capabilities: for an expert system to be successfully implemented and used it is necessary that the system performs at least almost as well as the expert in the field - since if it does not then it is not worth implementing the system. It will obviously be desirable to have the system perform better than a human expert, but there are still benefits to be achieved if an "almost as good" system is distributed amongst a wide number of users.

Reasonable response time: This is very closely linked to the previous factor, if the system takes an unreasonable time between questions or providing answers then the system will not be used and end users will revert to the previous practice of asking the human expert for advice. When one designs a standard computer system it is necessary to obtain a criteria for response times and so systems analysis techniques can be used here.

Modifiability: Human expertise is changing all the time. New facts, techniques and methods are being devised, new tests and rules of thumb come to light. An expert system must provide the user with a similar level of flexibility as humans in modifying its knowledge base.

An active user interface: Work in systems analysis has shown that no matter how brilliant the technical solution to a problem, if the social aspects of the system - both on a personal level as is found in the user interface, and on an organisational level - are not dealt with properly the system will no be used. This fact has often been overlooked with some authors arguing that "the quality of the knowledge base is the ultimate determinant of the usefulness and effectiveness of the application". (Bryant,1988) This is simply not true - a brilliant knowledge base lumbered with a poor user interface will not be used, whilst a small knowledge base with a good interface may be very useful.

Software engineering principles: There is currently considerable debate as to whether the rapid prototyping system development methodology should be used or not. We believe that it should be used, but that is should only be used for prototyping, not for the real system. The use of prototypes can be very useful for helping the expert out of *meta-unknowing* (not knowing what he doesn't know). These prototypes, however, should not be used as the final runtime system since they generally have not been developed using proper software engineering principles.

1.2.3 Advantages and disadvantages

Well written expert systems can have a number of advantages over the manual human system. These include:

Availability: If the knowledge of an expert is stored on a file then it is possible to distribute this information widely around the organisation - one copy could exist in each area that requires it. Furthermore this copy would always be available, there would be no problems about waking up the expert in the middle of the night etc.

Consistency: As we described earlier, human experts can have "off" days, they can make biased decisions for all sorts of reasons. An expert system, on the other hand, will always produce the same solution for the same problem (if the knowledge base remains unchanged).

The main disadvantages of expert systems are now described:

Selection of domain: Some areas of expert system application work well, others do not. As is the case with most computer based systems the decision whether or not to use a particular technique in a particular domain is an important one. The problems involved in selecting a domain suitable for expert system techniques is, ironically, an ideal expert system domain.

Testing: The testing of expert systems, especially in those domains where the system is being used to help make decisions rather than simply offering advice, are particularly critical in the need for tested systems. The user must be sure that the advice offered by the system is the best possible and takes into account all possible side effects. Ultimately, however, this is a question of responsibility - who is responsible ? the person who used the expert system, the person who wrote the expert system, the person whose knowledge is contained within the expert system or the person who authorised the use of expert systems. At the current time there have been no legal precedents set in this field.

Uncertainty: In the real world we do not deal only with true and false facts. We are often only certain to a particular degree, of a fact - we are 80% sure that we left the papers at home. Ideally an expert system should be able to cope with uncertainty. There is, however, a major theoretical problem finding valid statistical laws for use in the kind of probabilistic reasoning that expert systems must undertake.

Limitations: A human expert knows his limitations. A computer based system, unless it has been specifically programmed that way, does not.

Acceptability: The introduction of expert system technology into a firm will have serious consequences for the organisational set up of the firm. These factors will have to be taken into consideration when the use of expert systems is being considered otherwise the system may face active opposition from within the organisation.

Knowledge acquisition: By far the most serious problem for the development of expert systems is the "bottleneck" caused by knowledge acquisition. The process of eliciting and storing an expert's knowledge is often a long and slow process.

1.2.4 A word of caution

When one is dealing with expert systems it is easy to get carried away with the thought of a computer system that can solve all your problems by making it as intelligent as a human. Unfortunately this is not the case.

Authors such as Dreyfus & Dreyfus (Dreyfus & Dreyfus, 1986) have argued that artificial intelligence can never come about in the current paradigm of computer science. They argue that true human experts use knowledge that is above the level of facts and rules currently in use. This higher level knowledge makes use of patterns of characteristics that cannot be explicitly defined. For example the rules or facts needed to drive a car could never be stated explicitly since there are always new combinations of situations, road conditions, traffic densities etc. yet, a human driver can cope with driving down a new road as easily as an old road, since he can recognise higher level patterns and similarities than could be stated in the rules one uses for teaching. The argument continues that this higher level knowledge - the jump to intuitive thinking can only be brought about through practice and cannot be taught.

Another problem is described by Winograd and Flores (Winograd & Flores, 1986) who speak about the Speech Act theory of Austin (Austin, 1962) and Searle (Searle, 1969,1971). If someone who you have no reason to disbelieve says that *the sky is purple* a commitment has been made by the speaker that the facts as stated do exist (that the sky is in fact purple). Indeed if the sky was not purple, then you would expect there to be some reason as to why that person said it was - there would need to be some commitment or reason as to why it was so described - maybe the person said it for a joke, for example, otherwise the statement would not be seen as being made by a rational (intelligent) human. This commitment to the real world is not (cannot) be found in a computer that is simply moving electronic pulses from one place to another. Similarly if a human asks for your temperature there is a commitment on the part of the person making the request that he wants the information. Can this commitment exist on the part of a computer, how is the user to know whether the system really wants the user to provide their temperature, or if this is just a message thrown out by a badly written program?

The arguments just presented are arguments against the automation of full-scale human intelligence, so called *strong AI*. They do not, however, say that the use of some limited "knowledge based" technologies cannot be advantageous to a business organisation. To draw an analogy, the most complex industrial robots available today cannot mimic human manipulative skills at anything more than a very basic level, however, this does not mean that these robots have a useful place in some industrial processes. Provided that one has an understanding that expert systems are not the answer to all the problems, that they do have limitations and they can never work as well as a true intuitive expert then no problems should arise. In some areas, such as the "stimulus response" interactions for a diagnostic expert system for a machine, the causality that can be expressed in, for example, production rules, is sufficient to aid the user in the diagnostic task and an intuitive expertise, whilst possibly speeding up the task further, adds no major benefit to the process.

1.3 Models of Expert Systems

1.3.1 The simple Expert System Model

In describing models of an expert system we will start by introducing a simplified model of an expert system with only its most basic of features. This will then be extended to include the more advanced features found in current expert systems.

The simple expert system model consists of only four parts. These are the knowledge base, the inference engine, the user interface and the working memory. A diagrammatic way of representing the relationships between the different parts is shown in figure 1.1.

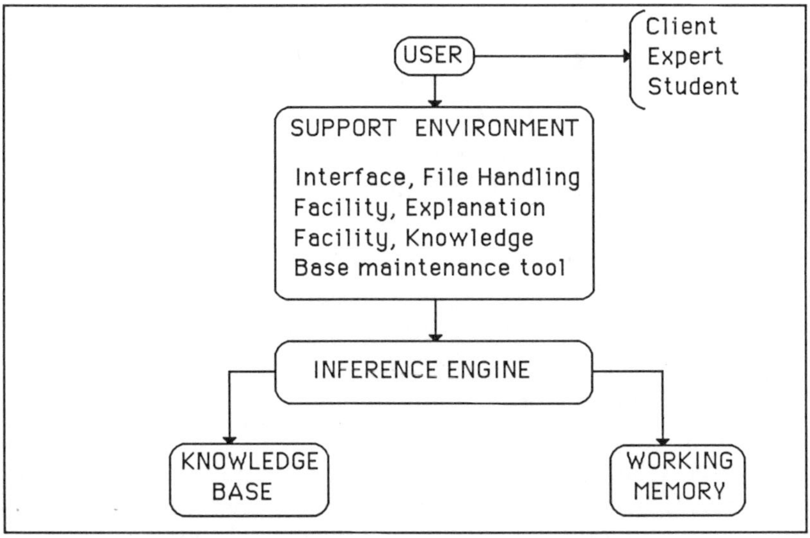

Figure 1.1 The simple Expert System Model

The knowledge base: An expert system makes use of the knowledge of an expert to provide the user with useful information about the domain. This knowledge is stored in a set of files known as the knowledge base or knowledge bank. The most common form of the knowledge is IF-THEN production rules.

The Inference engine: Just as a book is of no use without a reader, an knowledge base is of no use without an inference engine. An inference engine manipulates the knowledge in the knowledge base to provide new information. Typically in a production rule system, the inference engine uses some form of logical deduction to provide the answers.

The user interface: For the expert system to be of any use it must communicate with the user - this is either done directly via the screen and keyboard, or indirectly via external links to machines and monitoring devices etc.

Finally the working memory contains details of the state of the system's knowledge at a particular time. Thus at the start the working memory is empty, whilst part of the way through the interaction it will contain sets of facts which are known to be true and facts that are known to be false.

A typical interaction would involve the user calling up the expert system (through the user interface). The expert system then uses the inference engine to manipulate the rules in the knowledge base. If the system needs to know some facts, it will ask the user (again through the user interface) and then store these facts in the working memory. Any new facts that the inference engine derives are also stored in the working memory. This process continues until either the system provides the user with an answer to his query, or until there are no more rules that can be used.

1.3.2 The Environment Model

Expert systems that are currently available differ quite markedly from the traditional picture that has been described above. The differences lie not so much in the contents of the expert system rather they highlight the movement towards an integrated development environment, complete with an (implicit or explicit) development methodology. This model is shown is figure 1.2.

The first point to note is that the support environment is considerably larger than in the simple model - both in absolute size and relative importance. To further emphasise this point, the Dipmeter Expert System (which is an expert oil exploration model) the inference engine took up 8% of the total code, the knowledge base was 22% of the code, the user interface 42% and all the other parts of the support environment 28%. Similarly for PESYS (one of the expert system shells we describe later on), approximately 16% of the code was taken up in routines associated with the inference engine, the knowledge base was stored separately, but the code used to read it in took up 14%, the user interface was 25% of the code and other support facilities used 45% of the code.

In the current model, the knowledge base is split up into three distinct parts - the core knowledge about the domain (this is the only knowledge that was stored in the simple model), common sense knowledge and heuristic knowledge. Heuristics are facts about facts, whilst common sense knowledge is the unstated/assumed knowledge that is often ignored in knowledge elicitation for expert systems.

The support environment is now much more than simply a user interface and explanation facility. It now contains a sophisticated knowledge base maintenance tool, a knowledge base handling facility that deals with those items that have become standard on large scale database systems, for example security, data integrity, restart capabilities etc. An external interface is available to connect the expert system to conventional databases, simulation and statistical packages etc. The support environment may also contain a natural language processor, time mechanism, networking and distributed processing facilities as well as graphic and linguistic units.

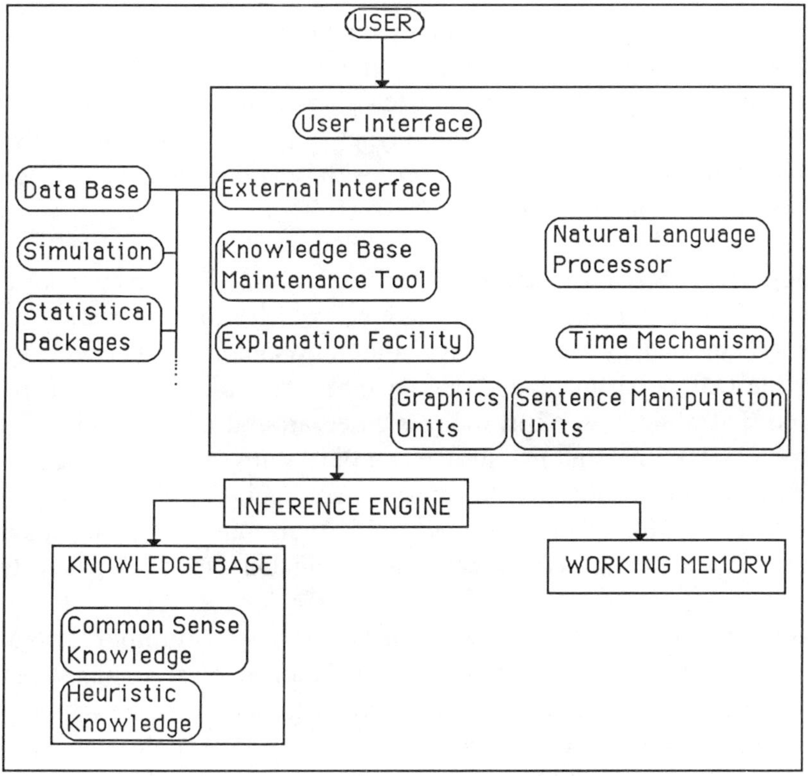

Figure 1.2 The Environmental Model

Whilst not all of these facilities are available on all the current expert systems we predict that these will form a basic minimum requirements list for future expert systems.

1.4 Expert System products

The expert systems market place is constantly developing, however some authors feel that it is possible to see the market developing into four main areas. (Land et al, 1988)

1.4.1 Tailor made systems

The applications of tailor made systems are often experimental and focus on organisational learning. As such they tend to be in-house projects, funded as acts of faith. Thus many projects are initiated by non technologists who have a belief in the power of the approach. Furthermore the fact that learning is the requirement tends to keep these types of project within the walls of a given organisation, reinforced by concern with the proprietary knowledge that such systems will contain.

Support for these observations comes from a PACTEL survey reported in Business Computing and Communications, which found that 27% of the expert systems activity reported was initiated by senior management, against 7% by the D.P. department, and of course 58% don't know! The survey also revealed that while most effort today is based around microcomputers (28% of respondents), mini and mainframe computers are seen as important, with considerable faith in this as the future route (mainframe 2% today, 18% projected for 1990). This would seem to further confirm the movement to integrate Expert System activity with main stream Data Processing activity.

Today we also see a limited, though increased number of "fully engineered" expert systems, often in technical or medical domains. A fully engineered system is one that has found a mainstream role in the organisation, contains many person years of development, and has been through a number of cycles of development. The classic example here is the DEC R1/XCON system.

In the future as expert systems prove their value, the rationale will move from learning to provide core systems designed to take their place in the general portfolio of D.P. systems, and undergo the management and financial control that comes with this move. The process is one that will put further emphasis on the role of D.P. departments as Information (or Knowledge) custodians, and perhaps hasten their move from technology managers to information managers.

1.4.2 Generic Systems

Recently a market in Generic systems has emerged, otherwise known as "packaged" expert systems. The essence of a generic is that it is a true product, containing a knowledge base in a domain of general interest. Examples from the U.K. would include products that advise on employment law, welfare benefits and taxation. These tend to be built around domains of legislation and financial management, which attracts many potential users. The intention in general is to complement or replace the skills of professional advisors. At the same time in other areas, such as operational research, previously packaged "solutions", such as stock control, production planning and project management are recast in the mould of expert systems.

It is in the nature of the generic system, as defined above, that the knowledge base will be the principle attraction to the purchaser, and that the supplier will be expected to serve to keep it up to date. Thus we see here the start of the move from an industry based on software skills, to an industry based on knowledge or information. The generic will be used more as a reference tool than as a way to capture specific knowledge or skill. Thus these systems can be seen more as an extension to the printed page, than as an extension to the programmed procedure.

1.4.3 Knowledge Base

The third product, as yet only in its infancy, is the knowledge base itself. The existence of a market in knowledge is universally acknowledged, and largely multinational corporations are committed to exploiting it, and yet today we can identify only a few knowledge base products that are available separately from operational software. Expertech, a large U.K. shell developer, has entered into the knowledge base market selling knowledge bases to run with its software in domains such as employment law. One of the limitations to a wider market is clearly that there are no agreed standards for what a knowledge base should look like, though the emergence of dominant shell products and in particular production rule systems, might drive this process to a point equivalent to the ubiquitous Lotus 1-2-3 spreadsheet format. The enormous interest attracted to the Hypercard production on the Macintosh suggests perhaps the start of a general "knowledge" format.

1.4.4 Data processing systems incorporating intelligent elements

Most existing expert systems are stand alone systems with few if any linkages into the organisations data processing systems of data bases and programs. At the same time today's D.P. systems are primarily concerned with well structured, procedure defined applications. It is true that the D.P. community had developed its own form of rule based processing using devices like decision tables and decision table processors. However, in general the intelligence (knowledge) dealt with was of a very simple and well structured kind.

Using the new technology and concepts acquired from work in artificial intelligence, designers of standard D.P. applications will incorporate more intelligence into systems as an aid to users. Work in this direction is proceeding now. For example the next generation of spreadsheets will be intelligent spreadsheets, and the ESPRIT project is developing a project management work-bench which has intelligent features such as the capability of anticipating problems and advising the project manager that action to avoid the problems is needed.

Not only will the D.P. systems of the future incorporate increasing amounts of intelligence, they may well use techniques derived from the expert systems movement to carry out procedures which previously used conventional programming techniques. The knowledge incorporated in DEC's XCON expert system is the kind which has been used for many years in product explosion and production and material scheduling applications. By holding that knowledge, not in the form of the classic "product specification" data base, but in the form of deterministic rules, the designers of XCON have made significant gain in flexibility. As a result it has been possible for DEC product engineers to devise new methods of configuring and building VAX computers. These developments are reflected in the growth of the knowledge base from a few hundred rules, defining VAX configurations, to more than three thousand rules.

Thus the development of expert systems ideas within the D.P. community is twofold. One leading to the increased possibility of applications incorporating elements of intelligence. The second permitting D.P. systems to become flexible by using some of the new tools of expert system technology.

1.5 Summary

This chapter has introduced the notion of an expert system and has placed this within the wider field of Artificial Intelligence. We have defined some of the more important characteristics of an expert system and stated some of the advantages and disadvantages of the expert system approach. Finally we have suggested ways in which the future market for expert systems products will develop.

Chapter 2

Introduction to Knowledge Engineering

2.1 Introduction

Throughout the past two decades, Artificial Intelligence researchers have been learning to appreciate the great value of domain-specific knowledge as a basis for solving problems. Although computers have many advantages over humans, including speed and consistency, they cannot compensate for ignorance.

Knowledge engineering is the task of obtaining the know-how of an expert in a particular domain, often so that it may be used to compensate for the inherent ignorance of a computer. The interaction typically involves a "knowledge engineer" interacting with an expert (or number of experts) in order to "extract" their knowledge, rules of thumb and strategies for solving problems. In short, all those facilities that make them experts rather than just individuals who have read about the domain.

Four phases of knowledge engineering can be recognised :

- Selection of an appropriate domain
- The Knowledge elicitation process
- Coding the system
- Testing, debugging and refining the system

In this chapter we introduce criteria for selecting a domain and some of the techniques that can be used in the knowledge elicitation process. Some of these knowledge elicitation techniques are developed in chapter five, where an actual knowledge elicitation case study is described. The coding of the system, that is converting the knowledge elicited from the expert into a form that can be used in an expert system is described in chapter three.

The techniques for knowledge elicitation described in this chapter are based on (human) knowledge engineer and expert interaction. Mechanised tools whereby the expert effectively interacts directly with the computer are described in chapter four.

2.2 Selection of an appropriate problem

The selection of the right problem is probably the most critical part of the entire development effort. If an inappropriate problem is chosen, the entire effort may collapse as problems that no one foresaw affect the project.

The first stage of the selection process often begins with a review of the likely domains in which an expert system could be utilised. At this stage the expert and knowledge engineer are not likely to have been identified.

Suitable domains are characterised by the use of expert knowledge, judgement and experience. Recognised experts must exist in the domain and these experts must be better than average at performing the task. This expertise must also be available on a reliable and continuing basis.

A rule of thumb, that is often used to decide on the suitability of a domain is to ask whether human expert can solve the problem in between half an hour and two hours, over the telephone. The reasoning being that shorter problems are probably best solved using conventional methods. Problems that take more than two hours are probably too complicated. Similarly if the problem can only be solved with the expert applying a "hand's on" approach then it is likely that the actual solution to the problem will involve the sort of "holistic" "by-inspection" type of solution that cannot be automated by current expert systems techniques.

Once the project has been identified and authorised, usually by management, the knowledge engineer will start his preparatory work. An important first step, particularly if the use of expert systems is being "imposed" on the expert, is for the knowledge engineer (KE) to read up about the subject, understanding basic terminology and concepts. This information can often be found in text books, manuals and existing in-house documentation. Nothing is more likely to discourage a skeptical expert than having to spend the first few hours explaining the most basic concepts that even a beginner would know. Whilst this information is not the knowledge of the expert it allows the KE to identify key concepts used in the problem and may also indicate areas where the meanings used by an expert extend beyond those used in the text books. For example an expert may use the term "broken spring" to mean a spring that has completely broken and "spring that needs replacement" to signify a spring that has begun to perform erratically.

One other vital piece of preparation is for the KE to know the name, responsibility, position and job of the expert.

At the present time, the process involved in selecting a domain suitable for the use of expert system technology is primarily done on an ad hoc basis. There is clearly a need for further research to be done in this area.

2.3 The Knowledge Elicitation Process

The process of eliciting knowledge can, according to some, be split into two distinct areas - knowledge elicitation and knowledge acquisition. Knowledge elicitation is the process whereby the knowledge about the domain is obtained from the expert. Knowledge acquisition, on the other hand, is the process of converting the extracted knowledge into a form suitable for use in an expert system. This conversion of the knowledge is described in the next chapter. Here we discuss methods of obtaining the knowledge of the expert.

Many problems exist in knowledge elicitation. Prerequisites include an expert who is both co-operative and articulate, a knowledge engineer who knows about computers, artificial intelligence, psychology, diplomacy, expert systems and a whole range of other social skills.

The process of acquiring knowledge is very labour intensive and it takes a considerable period of time. Add to this the fact that in many cases there is only one expert and one knowledge engineer involved in the process and a considerable "bottleneck" can arise.

One possible model of the knowledge acquisition process divides it into two stages - the initial structuring of the domain and the actual knowledge collection.

2.3.1 The initial structuring of the domain

During this stage of knowledge acquisition, both the expert and the knowledge engineer will determine the important features of the problem (for example type and scope of the problem, additional experts if needed, time and computing facilities etc.) and the goals or objectives of building the expert system.

It is important that this stage of the design is undertaken properly since the decisions about the type and scope of the problem and the model used to solve it affect the success of the overall project. (See chapter 3. section 3.1). Unfortunately many experts solve problems without having a good model of how they do it.

In this stage it is also important that the knowledge engineer and domain expert form a good working relationship since they are likely to be working together for at least a few months.

There is no specific methodology for getting the basic structure of the domain but one solution is that they should aim to produce a handbook containing - a general problem description, a bibliography of reference documents, a glossary of terms, a list of experts in the field, some reasonable performance metrics and descriptions of typical reasoning scenarios. Ideally this document should contain all the information "that the expert would want to know if he was starting in the domain again". It may also be useful to hold a series of meetings with the expert so that the assumptions and attitudes that lie behind the expert's thinking can be examined in detail.

One other approach that may well prove to be useful in the initial structuring of the domain is to decide on the approach that the expert uses in his problem solving strategy. Does he use a method that works from symptoms and finds the possible effects that could result, or does he work from a number of possible results and tries to justify them.

It is at this stage that various problems with experts first come to light. (Welbank, 1983) (Hart, 1986).

- *The unenthusiastic expert*. In some cases experts are reluctant to take part in the project. This may be because they feel that the project has no chance of succeeding. Alternatively they may feel threatened by the prospect of the tool taking over their jobs. The knowledge engineer must ensure that the expert will not lose interest and deliberately make himself unavailable etc.

If the expert is skeptical about the chance of the project succeeding then a number of techniques can be used. Moore (1987), states that in B.P. inductive tools are used to find underlying structure behind the expert's decision making and can demonstrate that an automated system may work in this domain. This "ten minute test" of the expert should be enough to gain his interest, otherwise they feel that the project is unlikely to succeed. In any case it is vital that the expert is given early feedback so that he can see that his efforts are productive.

An expert who has groundless fears for his job security can be persuaded by redefining the domain that the expert system is to tackle. By using participative methodologies the expert system can be targeted at those areas of the problem that the expert does not enjoy doing, leaving the more interesting work to the human specialist. For example if 80 per cent of the problems can be solved easily then it may be useful to put these problem solving abilities into the expert system, leaving the remaining 20 per cent of difficult but stimulating problems to the expert. This approach has the added advantage that the actual implementation is more likely to be complete and workable.

Other possible techniques for keeping the expert's enthusiasm alive include holding group discussions, having experts criticise each other, having "knowledge competitions" and examining one problem in depth.

- *The inaccessible expert.* An expert who continually fails to make or cancels appointments may well be facing the problems outlined above. In this case the knowledge engineer must try and solve the underlying problem. This problem can also arise if an expert is willing and able to participate in the project, but if he has a supervisor who is not amenable to losing his top expert for a period of time - again the reasons for this may be similar to those discussed above.

- *The inarticulate expert*. Problems arise when experts cannot state their knowledge when asked. Psychological experiments have shown that people are, in general, not very aware of their own reasoning. Furthermore, the more expert they are, the less aware of it (Dreyfus & Dreyfus, 1986). The expert may not be able to say anything about how he reasons, or what he says is incomplete or even wrong. One possible partial solution to this problem is for the knowledge engineer to deliberately make an error in his understanding of the expert. It is often easier to criticise a wrong move than it is to make a right one. Thus by deliberately making wrong moves, the knowledge engineer allows the expert to overcome his inarticulation. Naturally this deliberate error making has to be kept within reasonable limits.

- *Discourtesy*. Obviously problems will arise if the expert develops a dislike or subconscious fear of the knowledge engineer. The knowledge engineer should seek to maintain a good personal relationship with the expert at an early stage of the process.

2.3.2 The actual knowledge base collection

The problems in this area are particularly associated with those of question design. Even if the expert has conscious access to his knowledge, getting at it is slow if he is asked the wrong questions and much easier if the questions are specific.

There are two basic approaches to finding out what experts know - Interviewing the expert about the field and observing him solving the problem.

2.3.3 The interview approach

Interview data tends to be at the level of rules and general principles, and cannot produce the detailed context of real behaviour. On the other hand, interviews are the best means of extracting background knowledge and reasons behind behaviour. They are also faster than observational methods.

We now list the various questioning strategies in use today:

Critical incident

This is a technique, first described by Flanagan (Flanagan, 1954) and much used in applied psychology. The method asks the expert to select particularly memorable events and then detail their actual experiences. The method assumes that the memory of particularly difficult or remarkable cases is most likely to be kept accurately and he will find them interesting to discuss. However, there is also a considerable chance that the expert will, after the event, reinterpret his decisions to reduce his cognitive dissonance, to justify the action he took. There is also a problem, however, that the expert may digress.

Repertory Grid

The repertory grid has been developed by the psychologist Kelly (Kelly, 1955). It is a representation of the expert's view of a particular problem. It is composed of constructs and elements. A construct is a bipolar characteristic which each element has to some degree, for example shape, weight, dimension. The typical procedure begins by collecting a set of objects in the domain of the grid. About ten objects are normally collected. They are then presented in threes and the expert is asked to say in what way two of the three are alike and different form the third. As all the possible combinations of three are presented, the ways in which objects in the fields are distinguished form one another becomes clear.

The results of the repertory grid are, by their very nature, subjective and the technique becomes unmanageable with more than about ten objects.

Reclassification

The method is based on the idea that an expert may find it easier to work backwards from a goal rather than forwards from a set of symptoms. The method reclassifies each goal into a set of facts that provided evidence for it, and reclassifies those facts until it reaches the facts which could be directly observed by the expert.

Distinguishing the goals

Given a specific goal, the expert can be asked to specify the sets of evidence which are necessary and sufficient to distinguish this goal from the other alternatives. The method results in a structured model of the expert's knowledge. The method provokes discussion about the precise nature of and reasons for the goals.

Dividing the domain

This method, similar to reclassification, works in reverse. Instead of starting with the goals, the expert starts by describing symptoms and successively groups them until he reaches the final goal.

2.3.4 Observational techniques

An alternative approach to asking the expert what he does is to watch him as he solves a problem. A list of techniques that are based on this approach is provided. They are often called protocol analysis, but not all of them have the characteristics of true protocol analysis.

Protocol analysis

Here the expert is asked to explain what he is doing in the actual process of carrying out his job. A tape or video recording is collected and later transcribed and analysed. In true protocol analysis (Newall & Simon, 1972) the problem solver only describes his thoughts or impressions; he does not try to explain them.

The method has the advantage that the task situation is completely natural and the task can be done exactly as it normally is. Another advantage of the method is that the study can be run without taking up much of the expert's time.

The method also has disadvantages. Protocols collected on the job do not cover every situation that could arise. The expert cannot verbalise as fast as he reasons, which makes for important deficiencies in the type of material collected.

In short, protocol analysis is a skilled and difficult task. It is also very time consuming, partly because the protocol is sketchy but also because it is laborious to collect recordings without doing analysis on the spot.

Forward scenario simulation

With this method the expert chooses a very elementary scenario and "walks through" the reasoning to reach a goal. It has difficulties when having to deal with unwieldy rules.

Procedural simulation

Here the domain specialist is required to solve a specific problem in a normal manner and setting. He is asked to reason about specific events, then justify his reasoning and detail all the steps that led to a conclusion. When the rules have been formulated, he is asked whether they are generally true, or true only in some contexts. However, simply asking why the expert has come to a particular conclusion, may not be very helpful.

2.4 Testing and evaluating the knowledge that has been elicited

At the present time few methods have been documented for testing and evaluating a knowledge base. Rigorous testing is fairly uncommon with the final running system and there is even less testing of the knowledge that has been elicited (O'Keefe et al., 1987).

Current knowledge testing is based on the analysis of the implications of the knowledge elicited. For example, using cluster analysis on the repertory grid results may produce levels of similarity - this concept is fairly closely related to this other concept - and these can then be checked using "intuition". An example of this form of testing is presented in the case study given in chapter 5.

Other forms of validation, which are generally used once the knowledge has been written into an expert system, include giving the system a number of test cases and comparing the accuracy of its results with that of an expert. Problems obviously arise when it comes to defining successful and unsuccessful solutions. This is often a subjective decision and the result is dependent on the choice of test cases. It is important to note that if the system is tested using examples that were used to create the knowledge for the system, or if the original expert is used for the comparison with the system's performance, the results are unlikely to hold considerable respect.

Predictive tests can be used when a problem is given to an expert and a system. The expert then predicts the outcome of the diagnosis and this is compared with the actual outcome.

Turing Tests or blind tests are arranged so that experts are given a test case and a report on it and are asked to judge whether the report was generated by an expert system or a human. Clearly this method reduces the bias of the validation. Statistical tests may be used on the results to see if there is any variation between those diagnosis that were produced by humans and those produced by the system.

Field tests arise when the system is tested in the application site. Errors are reported as they occur and are corrected. This process continues until the system's performance is at an acceptable level.

2.5 A knowledge engineer's characteristics and guidelines for his work

The following list will give an idea of the optimal person's talent and the ways they are likely to be needed in the knowledge engineering process. It is unlikely that a knowledge engineer would have all these qualities, but as it is certain that the selection of the knowledge engineer will have a crucial effect on the success of a project, it is useful for the management to explore the task required of the knowledge engineer.

Good communication skills

As well as the effective use of the spoken and written word, the knowledge engineer must also be able to interpret body language. The knowledge engineer, in order to ensure the commitment of the expert to the development, must first establish a good relationship between himself and the expert.

Tact and diplomacy

The knowledge engineer must understand that, because so much of the expert's knowledge is intuitive and subconscious, at times there is as much to be learned form rambling as from asking direct questions. An expert who has been alienated by thoughtless and tactless treatment will tend to lose interest. Any suggestion that the expert system in development will replace or outperform the expert can be disastrous.

Intelligence

The knowledge engineer must keep up-to-date with advances in hardware and software. He must be able to learn about a new knowledge domain and understand enough of the terminology and principles to be able to discuss it fully with an acknowledged expert.

Patience

The knowledge engineer and expert must work together as a team, each respecting the other. This often requires patience as he comes to understand the reasons for the expert's hesitancy etc.

Persistence

The knowledge engineer must retain his enthusiasm and belief in the project and despite and despite any setbacks he must always persist in the conviction that success will come.

Logicality

Knowledge engineering experience shows that if you just ask experts how they do something, what often happens is that they tell you what they believe is the procedure. If the knowledge engineer then watches the expert in action, it turns out that they do something slightly differently. It also happens that the experts do not follow a step-by-step analysis. The knowledge engineer therefore needs to be able to argue reasonably, recognising valid statements and providing meaningful counter-examples for possible errors. All of the above require a level of clear though and logicality on behalf of the knowledge engineer.

Programming knowledge

It is advisable that the knowledge engineer understands programming and the various forms of knowledge representation available.

Finally the knowledge engineer must have versatility and inventiveness since problems will arise that have not been covered so far.

2.6 Problems with knowledge elicitation

Poulymenakou and Doukidis (1988) identify two dimensions of complexity in the knowledge elicitatio task. At the present time it is more of an art than a craft. There is no theoretical background that would serve as a general reference framework and would aid planning and executing knowledge elicitation and evaluating the results.

The second factor is the inaccessibility of the expertise. On the one hand, experts are a scarce resource, difficult to co-operate with, even when they are found. Reporting their thinking is alien to them and it is hard to maintain their interest in a case. Moreover the elicited data often contains omissions or inconsistencies. Finally, human expertise may prove to be inaccessible.

2.7 Summary

This chapter has introduced a number of different techniques for knowledge elicitation. Whilst each technique has its own advantages and disadvantages, it must always be borne in mind that the process of elicitation aims at obtaining the information that the expert has and the methods he uses for solving problems, rather than eliciting the knowledge that the expert thinks he has and the description of the methods he uses in the process.

There is a considerable overlap between the work of cognitive psychology, systems analysis and knowledge elicitation but it is important to bear in mind the objectives and assumptions of the particular methods used. For example, systems analysis may uncover a description of how a problem is solved whereas an expert system would need to mimic the actual method used, not its description.

Chapter 3

Representing the Knowledge

3.1 Understandable Knowledge Representations

Human Experts solve problems by using things that they know about the domain (In chapter 1 we presented some arguments against the idea of being able to store the knowledge of an expert in a machine, however for the sort of problems that current expert systems are aimed at, and the sort of level of competence that is expected from them, the following discussion is still valid). This "information" exists in a number of different forms - there are facts about a domain - Minis are a kind of car - there are connections between items in a domain - a flat battery and the fact that a car won't start are connected - and there are "heuristics" or "rules of thumb" - if there is a smell of petrol then it is probably best to examine the carburettor first.

In order to solve a problem or do some other useful work in a particular domain it is necessary to "know" something about the domain. One interpretation about how the knowledge about a domain can be structured is based on a decision analysis viewpoint. This method (Humphreys 1984,1988) divides the knowledge into five levels according to how much of the problem domain has been specified.

The top level of analysis (level 5) is where the problem or knowledge is expressed rather than encoded. At this level the domain is described and problem areas are noted - for example it is felt that area X is not working properly. The results of the search are used to direct the analysis at the lower levels described above. Due to its very nature level 5 analysis cannot easily be formalised.

In the fourth level of analysis the decision maker decides which type of representation techniques are to be used. Very often these techniques can be described in the decision makers own language rather than using formal specifications. Thus at this level of analysis the user may choose to use a multiple attribute analysis technique.

The third level of analysis is concerned with representing the knowledge in a particular structure. Thus if, for example, it has been decided to represent the knowledge using multiple attributes, analysis at level 3 will decide which attributes are to be used.

Level 2 analysis, also known as sensitivity analysis is typically characterised by the term *what-if ?*. By altering the "values" of the different types of knowledge it is possible to explore different hypotheses about the structure (opinions and views, etc.) rather than the structures themselves. Thus at this level the decision maker will explore the different attributes by altering their values.

The lowest level (level 1) is the one where one makes the "best assessment" of the likelihood of one of the predefined events that has been formulated at higher levels. This "best assessment" may be a subjective decision or an objective one based on predefined conditions.

Level of Analysis	Comparison with Knowledge Acquisition
5	Decide to use Expert Systems technology Obtain verbal information from Expert.
4	Select a knowledge representation.
3	Select variables/values to be used within the representation.
2	Specify knowledge according to different values within the representation.
1	Weight the rules.

By using this analysis it is easy to see where the problems arise if one decides on using a particular expert system before one has described and analysed the problem. A particular expert system shell will have made the decisions for levels 5 and 4 already and the user will be left with manipulations at levels 1, 2 and 3. If the representation chosen at level 4, however, is not suitable for the particular domain then the work done at the lower levels will be done in vain.

When one comes to representing the knowledge of the expert there are two conflicting aims that must be met. On the one hand the knowledge should be described in a form appropriate to the expert - the knowledge should be "understandable" to the expert on the other hand it should be in a machine processable form.

There are a number of important reasons why the knowledge should be stored in a form that is understandable by the expert. The first reason is that it simplifies the process of recording the knowledge that the expert imparts. The mere act of speaking has a number of problems - does the hearer hear the same words as the speaker speaks - "It isn't easy to wreck a nice beach" OR "It isn't easy to recognise speech" (Dreyfus & Dreyfus, 1986). In view of these difficulties it is best not to add further problems that are brought about because each participant in the knowledge acquisition process is a different human being. Each therefore has a different background and beliefs and so the interpretations they make of words, phrases and sentences can heavily influence their understanding of that speech even if that speech has been correctly heard.

If one uses a knowledge format that the expert can easily understand (i.e. not one in which he has to learn a special notation or set of keywords for) then the expert can verify the knowledge that they have given to the knowledge engineer. Provided that the representation technique is still understandable it is possible for the expert to verify a more formalised form of the knowledge. For example if the expert says *The case rests on the the tyre prints on the floor* and the knowledge engineer interprets this as *The packing container lies upon the marks made by a vehicle on the ground* then the expert can immediately agree or disagree with the interpretation.

A direct and important next step from the verifiability of the understandable knowledge representation is the fact that if the expert understands the knowledge then he is far more likely to accept being responsible for the knowledge. Having some agent taking responsibility for the knowledge used in an expert system is a vital step towards the widespread commercial use of expert systems (Stamper, 1988). Clearly no expert will take responsibility for some knowledge if he cannot even understand the form that it is presented in.

The conflicting aim of knowledge representation for computer based expert systems, however, is that the knowledge will have to be used in a computerised system and so the knowledge representation used will have to be in a computable form. Unfortunately in most cases these twin goals are incompatible. The representations described below make some effort towards making the knowledge representation understandable, but their primary role is in making the representation computable.

Attempts to make, for example, frames more "understandable" by giving the slots meaningful names still run into problems since many of these names are abbreviations invented by the programmer, often based on the abbreviations used by the knowledge engineer. Similarly the "fat predicates" of Prolog are only more-meaningful invented names and problems still arise if different programmers use different names for similar predicates. (Stamper, 1987,1988)

3.2 Computable knowledge representations

In the rest of this chapter we describe some of the more common means of representing "knowledge" in a computer (computable form) - semantic networks, object-attribute-value triplets, frames and rules. All of these techniques, except rules, make use of a principle known as inheritance to reduce the amount of information that needs to be stored. We will now describe inheritance.

3.2.1 Inheritance

Suppose we are concerned with a domain which contains a number of people. Each person in that domain has a number of facts associated with them:

John has two arms and two legs
Mary has two arms and two legs
Peter has two arms and two legs
Jane has two arms and two legs

This is shown in figure 3.1.

Figure 3.1 The domain before using inheritance

If we want to store all this information about each person then we will need a lot of memory - and a lot of information will be duplicated. It would clearly be more efficient to store all the common information once and have each person access it. The inheritance principle works in this way. If we declare that a person has two arms and two legs and then add that :

John is a person
Mary is a person
Peter is a person
Jane is a person

we can convey the same information, see figure 3.2

If we want to know how many arms and legs Jane has then we can "inherit" the values from the more general description of a person. It is not necessary for this inheritance to be restricted to only one level.

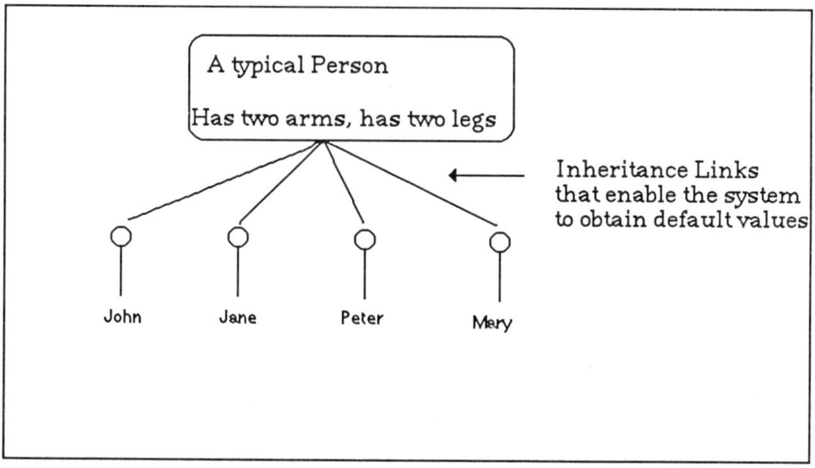

Figure 3.2 The Domain using Inheritance

Consider: *Fido is a dog*
Fido can fetch the paper
Dog is a kind of animal
Dogs have four legs
Animals can move

Figure 3.3 shows this.

If we want to know if Fido can fetch the paper the fact is immediately available, if we want to know how many legs Fido has then we have to inherit a value from the fact that Fido is a dog. Finally if we want to know if Fido can move we have to inherit the answer through Dog and Animal.

The most immediate problem with inheritance is that exceptions are handled very awkwardly. How is a system to cope if Fido unfortunately only has three legs.

One possible solution is to have the information placed at the level of Fido :
Fido has three legs

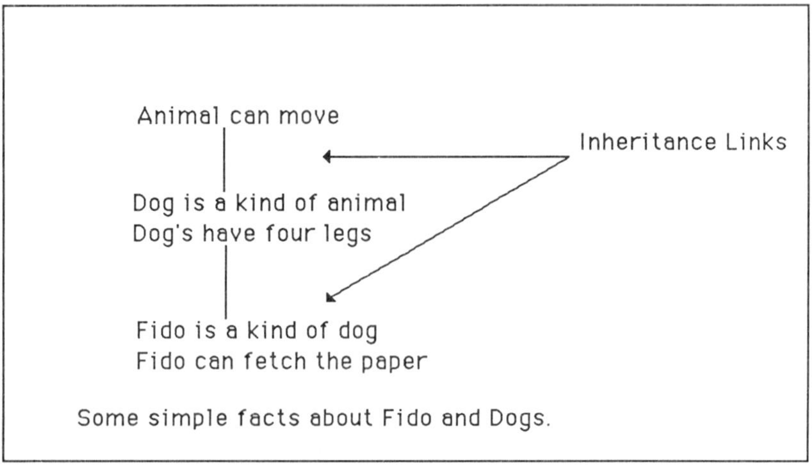

Figure 3.3 Multi-Level Inheritance

The system would therefore not inherit the value of four legs from the more general category. This, however, leads us onto the next problem - suppose we have the piece of information *Dogs eat dogfood* and we want to add the fact that Fido enjoys eating roast chicken as well as dogfood. If we were simply to add the fact:

Fido eats roast chicken

then the inheritance principle used for the previous problem would mean that the fact that Fido eats dogfood would not be inherited. (Otherwise we would also derive the fact that Fido has three and four legs!). Alternatively we could add the fact that Fido eats roast chicken and dogfood. Whilst this means that the system does work, it will cause problems if dogs eat a large list of items and this will also be very inefficient in terms of memory usage.

The solution is to add some flag at the end of the Fido statement that tells the system to continue to inherit the other values:

Fido eats roast chicken and continue

In this case Fido would have three legs (since the statement did not say continue) whilst he would eat roast chicken and dogfood.

3.2.2 Semantic Networks

The first type of knowledge representation technique that utilises inheritance is the semantic network or net. In a semantic network there are *nodes* and these nodes are connected by arcs known as *links*. Whilst there is no absolute constraint on the method of representing the information the following norm is quite widely accepted.

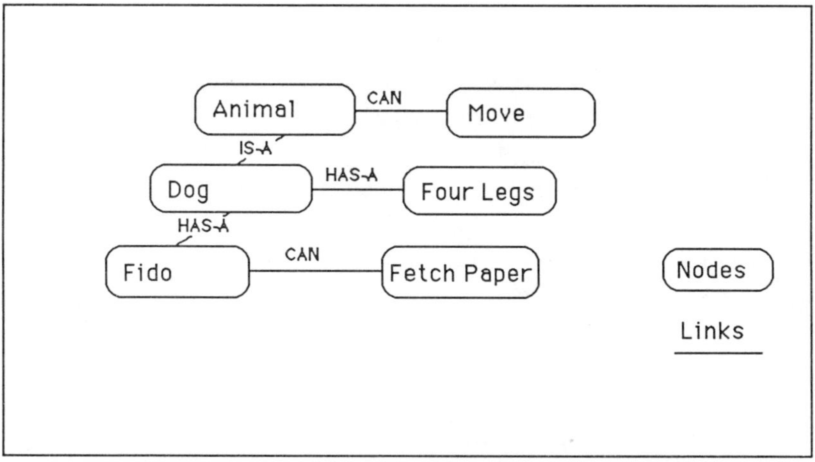

Figure 3.4 A simple Semantic Network

Nodes represent objects and descriptors. In the previous example nodes would include Fido, dog, fetch the paper, animal, move etc. The "objects" described are not necessarily physical objects - for example fetch the paper and move are not physical objects.

Links between nodes are used to show the relationship between the objects. Thus in the previous example we might have the links is-a, is-able-to/can and has-a etc. The resulting semantic network is shown in figure 3.4.

This example shows two of the most common forms of link - the IS-A link and the HAS-A link. The IS-A link is used to define the inheritance mechanism. A particular node can inherit information from any nodes that it is linked to with IS-A links. HAS-A links, on the other hand, connect attributes of nodes to other nodes thus the ability to fetch the paper is an attribute of Fido.

The major advantage of semantic networks are that new nodes and links can be created at any time - although unfortunately this means that there is no standardised way of describing the facts. This means that if two descriptions of facts are made they are not likely to be very similar.

3.2.3 Object-Attribute-Value triplets

Another very common form of knowledge structure is the OAV triplet. This can be thought of as storing the knowledge according to what it is about, what kind of knowledge it is and what its value is.

The fact that Fido has four legs would be classified as :

Object - Fido is the object in question
Attribute - Number of legs.
Value - Four.

Object	Attribute	Value
Fido	Number-of-legs	Four

There is an obvious link here between OAV triplets and semantic networks since the objects and values in OAV triplets match the nodes in a semantic network whilst an attribute matches the link between them. Since there is such an obvious link between them it is very easy to implement inheritance in OAV triplets.

If one is considering uncertain information then it is possible to extend the triplets to include certainty. These Object-Attribute-Value-Certainty quadruplets may look like this:

Object	Attribute	Value	Certainty
Fido	Age	8 Years	.8

The certainty factor (often a probability) is based on our belief in the facts being stated - in the previous example we are eighty per cent sure that Fido is 8 years old.

One final extension of the OAV triplet arises when one is only considering one object. Here it is not necessary to describe the object (since only one object exists). In all other respects the attribute-value pairs are identical to OAV triplets.

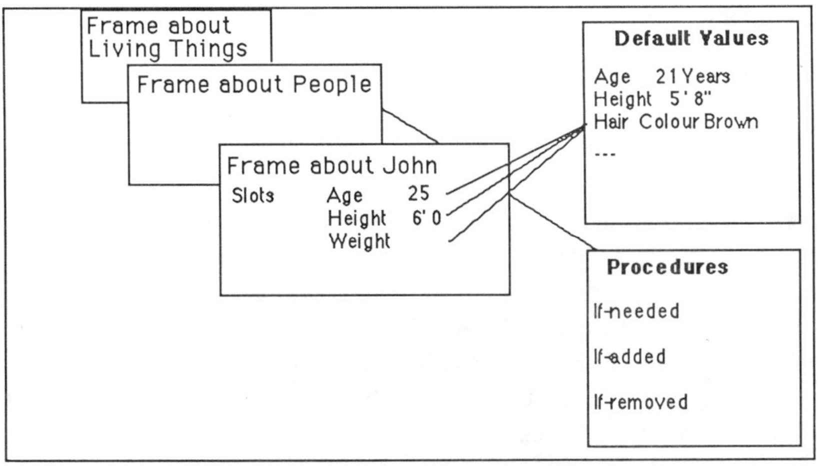

Figure 3.5 A heirarchy of Frames

3.2.4 Frames

Frames continue the ideas that have been developed so far, but present them in a far more structured way. Another important feature to note is that Frames were first implemented in LISP since LISP and its derivatives have many structures that can assist in the creation of frames.

One frame is used to describe one object and this object can either be a particular instance (as in a frame describing Fido) or it can be a particular type (as in a frame describing Dog). The different attributes of the frame are stored in *slots*, thus we have slots for the age of Fido, slots for the weight of Fido, his number of legs etc. What differentiates frames from the other data structures described previously is that a slot is not restricted to one item of data. A slot may contain the actual value, a default value, some program code to be run if a value is required or some program code to be run if a value is added. This ability to do a number of different things with slot values contribute greatly to the power of frames. Consider a frame describing a person called John:

Frame	Slots	Contents
John		
	IS-A	Person
	Age	Default 21, Actual 22
	Weight	IF added check valid weight
	Height	Default 5' 8"
	Hair Colour	Actual Brown
	Hobbies	IF needed read database

This frame contains a number of different slots (IS-A, Age, Weight, Height, Hair Colour, Hobbies) and each slot has a number of different values. For example the slot Age has a default value (21) and an actual value (22). The weight slot has a procedure attached to it (this is known as procedural attachment) and this procedure is called whenever a value is added. In this particular case the procedure checks that the weight is within certain reasonable limits. The hobbies slot also contains a procedure - in this case the procedure is called if a value is required to fill the slot. Other slots (such as hair colour) would use the default value (Brown) or use inheritance to obtain the value, but in cases like hobbies a procedure will be called which in this case obtains the data from a database. See figure 3.5 above.

A further extension of the frame principle is that of scripts. If a frame refers to an object, then a script refers to a sequence in time. Consider :

The cinema was showing "A room with a view". John paid his money. He enjoyed it very much.

Without some knowledge of the basic idea of visiting a cinema a computer system would not be able to answer questions like :

What did John do?
Which film did John go and see?
What did he enjoy doing?

A script about visiting the cinema would have slots that include - film to be seen (A room with a view), Enjoy (Watching film), Pay money (If added then Person has watched film).

3.2.5 Predicate Logic

The final method that is commonly used to represent knowledge is logic. Whilst courses that teach logic start off with an explanation of propositional logic, this form is not sophisticated enough to attempt to deal with a "real world" situation that would require the use of an expert system.

Propositional logic works by taking sentence parts and giving them truth values, they are combined using logistical connectives - AND, OR, NOT, IF AND ONLY IF, IMPLIES. For example *The sky is blue and the sea is green* might be represented as :

P - The sky is blue
Q - The sea is green

With the sentence being represented as *P and Q*. The limitations of propositional logic arise when one considers the deduction :

All men are mortal
John is a man
therefore John is mortal

Under propositional logic this is represented as

P - All men are mortal
Q - John is a man
R - John is mortal

There are, however, no laws of propositional logic that can prove the intuitively valid statement: *P and Q Implies R.* There is simply not enough power within the logic. For this reason predicate logic is used. Predicate logic works along the principle of quantifiers. Universal quantifiers are those that state ALL ... so the first sentence is based on a universal quantifier about men , whilst existential quantifiers are those that state at least one .... .

Predicates arise when one applies a particular property - P to some particular individual x. Therefore if P is the property of being a man and b is John the combination P(b) means that John has the property of being a man. If we use P for the property of being a man, Q for the property of being mortal and x as a variable then the three clauses above can be written as

ALL xs If P(x) then we imply Q(x)
For all things x, if x is a man then we imply that x is mortal.
P(John)
John is a man
Therefore Q(John)
Therefore John is mortal

Various laws of logic exist that allow us to manipulate these logical descriptions to obtain the desired results.

3.3 Production Rules

The most common form of knowledge representation, however, is that of the production rule. In its simplest form a production rule is simply a list of IF clauses followed by a list of THEN clauses:

IF it is raining
and I am not wearing a coat
THEN I will get wet

It has been argued that much of human intelligence can be represented in the form of IF-THEN rules. Whilst we believe that this is a considerable step to take, it is possible that a part of the intelligence required to solve problems can be expressed in rule form. On one extreme we have the formal "rules" that exist as part of the legislation of the country - *IF you are travelling on a motorway THEN you must not drive faster than 70 Miles Per Hour*. Social rules include examples like : *IF you meet a friend THEN it is polite say hello*. On a far more basic level there are the physical laws *IF two magnets have like poles together THEN they repel each other*.

3.3.1 Different types of rules

Production rules can come in three different forms - passive, active and semi-active. Passive rules are simply considered as lines of text. For example

IF the sky is blue
THEN it is unlikely to be raining

The inference engine makes no attempt to "understand" the content of the rules, it is simply treats them as lines of text and stores them as such. Passive rules are generally found in the simpler expert system models although for certain diagnostic type domains, where the system is guiding the expert in the real world, they may be sufficiently powerful. For example, if the human user is the one who is to find out whether a particular component is working, it is sufficient for the system to display the task to be undertaken.

Passive rules are very easy to implement in most programming languages, especially symbolic languages like LISP - as a string or array of characters, for example, and they can easily be manipulated as wholes.

Active rules are the direct opposite of passive rules. For example

((IF
(FUNCTION LESS-THAN Get-Age-Value Get-Minimum-Age))
(THEN
(FUNCTION OUTPUT 'You cannot buy alcohol legally, you are too young')))

When the inference engine uses active rules it manipulates the actual contents of the rules, in this case by calling predefined functions less-than and output, and so it can be thought of as "understanding" the rules, to the extent that it relates the contents of the rules to the real world (or at least part of its own program code). Active rules are more difficult to implement since they need to have the code written for each of the clauses. They are therefore more suitable for embedded expert systems and systems that obtain their own data rather than having the user provide the data for them.

Semi-active rules lie between the extremes of passive and active rules. For example

IF
The age IS-LESS-THAN 18
THEN
The person is too young to legally buy alcohol.

In this example rule the if part is partly active, to the extent that it has keywords that relate to program code. The rest of the clause and the then part of the rule is passive. There is, for example, no active part of the rule to obtain the age of the person, this is assumed to be a passive part. Semi-active rules are the most common form of rule found on current expert systems.

3.4 Manipulating the knowledge

Given that we have managed to convert our knowledge into rule format (this is by no means an easy step - indeed it may be the most difficult part of the development of expert systems) how does the system manipulate these rules (whether they are passive, active or semi active) to generate information? The part of the Expert System that manipulates the rules is normally known as the Inference Engine since this is the part of the program that Infers information from rules.

Two of the most common methods for inferencing information will now be described. These are *FORWARD CHAINING* and *BACKWARD CHAINING*. For both of these sets we will be using the following sets of rules:

IF E AND C THEN F
IF A THEN C
IF B THEN D
IF D THEN A

3.4.1 Forward Chaining

Before examining the theory behind forward chaining, consider the above rules in conjunction with the fact that B and E are true. Is it possible to derive that F is also true?

The answer to this is yes. It now becomes necessary to describe how this was done - the method described is forward chaining.

Forward chaining works by taking all the true facts and examining each rule to see if all the if parts of the rule are true. If they are then all the then parts are also true (by the principle of modens ponens). With this new extended list of true facts the process is repeated until either a suitable goal has been derived or no more information can be discovered.

In our previous example :

IF E AND C THEN F   Rule ignored since not all if parts are known
IF A THEN C   Rule ignored since if parts are not known
IF B THEN D Rule is used (*Fired*) and D is added to the knowledge base
IF D THEN A Rule is fired and A is added to the knowledge base

IF E AND C THEN F   Rule ignored since not all if parts are known
IF A THEN C   Rule is fired and C is added to the knowledge base
IF B THEN D Rule has already been used
IF D THEN A Rule has already been used

IF E and C THEN F Rule is fired. No more rules left to prove so inference engine stops.

Forward chaining is also known as data-driven inferencing since the method will not work unless there is some data available to drive the inference procedure - when there is no (more) data the inference engine stops.

3.4.2 Backward Chaining

The alternative form of inferencing that is commonly found in expert systems is that of backward chaining. Whilst forward chaining works by simply applying data to rules and seeing what comes out, backward chaining tries to prove a particular rule. In the previous examples consider trying to prove F.

The first rule states that F can only be true if both E and C are true. How then does one prove E - it cannot be proven by using any other rules and so it must be asked directly of the user. The next clause to be proven is C. By examining the rules we can see that C can be proven using the second rule (since it appears in the then part of the rule). To prove C we need to prove A. This can be found as the then part of rule four, which in turn needs D to be true. This recursive idea of trying to prove one thing by proving others is repeated one last time as B is needed to prove D. There are no rules that can prove B so once again the user is asked.

3.4.3 Mixed chaining

As inference methods both forward and backward chaining have advantages - and disadvantages. It is important to note that in certain circumstances particular disadvantages may not be that important to the running of the system.

One of the main advantages of forward chaining is that it does not require that information is added in any particular order - this means that in systems that assist machine floor real-time systems data can simply be input directly into the expert system on the other hand, if the user is entering information "by hand" then the system can offer no assistance in directing the user to enter the required information.

Backward chaining, on the other hand, is entirely directed - it asks the user for specific items of information and it can usually "justify" why it requesting the information. The problems with backward chaining occur when the system has "heuristics" or "rules of thumb" that should prevent it from either asking irrelevant questions or asking the wrong questions. For example, if a system was trying to determine what animal you are describing then it would appear stupid if it asked questions about mammals once you had said the animal was covered in feathers! Unfortunately this sort of heuristic information cannot normally be used in backward chaining.

In those circumstances where the inference strategy being used cannot allow the disadvantages stated above, an alternative compromise strategy is possible. This involves using backward chaining as the main inference strategy whilst using forward chaining to provide the advantages of data driven inferencing.

3.5 Relating rules with other knowledge representations

It would appear from what we have described that our knowledge representation techniques are based on two completely separate ideas. On the one hand we have the description of facts using techniques such as semantic networks, object attribute value triplets and frames, and on the other we have production rules.

The two techniques are, however, more closely related than at first they seem. Consider a OAV triplets such as

John Hair-colour Brown
John Beard-colour Red-brown

It would be quite simple to combine these two facts into a rule if we were to separate the value from the object and attribute. Thus IF object-attribute is a particular value THEN some other object-attribute has a particular value.

IF
 John Hair-colour = Brown
THEN
 John Beard-colour = Red-brown

When the inference engine examines this rule it will look up its knowledge base under John and Hair-colour and examine the value to see whether it is brown or not. If it is the rule will be fired. If the value does not exist the user will be asked for it. Since the system would be asking for the value of a particular attribute, in this case hair-colour, it would be possible for the user to shown a list of possible values - blonde, brown, white etc. and be asked to select an appropriate one. If the rule is fired the appropriate OAV triplet will be added to the working memory.

Although it may appear, therefore, that the only knowledge representation technique that is being used in a system is rules, this is not necessarily the case. It is possible for the rules to make use of the power and flexibility of the other knowledge representation techniques whilst protecting the user from the detail of these techniques.

3.6 Modularity

One obvious quality of production systems is that the individual productions in the rule base can be added, deleted or changed independently. They behave much like independent pieces of knowledge. Changing one rule, although it may change the performance of the system, can be accomplished without having to worry about direct *effects on the other rules, since rules communicate only by means of the context data structures (looking to see if their conditions are satisfied in the context and then modifying the context); they don't call each other directly.*

(Barr & Feigenbaum, 1983)

This important principle of production rule systems is all too often ignored. A lot of the power of expert systems derives from the fact that the knowledge base is kept entirely separate from the inference engine. All of this power, however, is lost if the rules within the knowledge base are interrelated.

Once again we are relearning the rules of systems analysis. Almost every systems analysis technique makes an effort to minimise redundancy since considerable errors can arise if (when) the system is modified whilst redundancy still exists. This problem is heightened in a knowledge base that will be subject to constant revision in the light of new rules of thumb and other heuristics.

Put simply redundancy occurs whenever one item is defined twice. In a data processing environment redundancy occurs if one were to define, for example, a bill as containing a name, an address, a quantity and a total amount on two separate occasions, once for the shipping department and once for the finance department.

Suppose now that a new regulation is brought into being that states that bills must contain also a tax reference code. There is no guarantee in the system as it stands that *both* definitions of bill will be altered accordingly. This problem is worsened if instead of only two definitions there are a large number of definitions. The data processing solution to these problems is to have one definition of bill and have the two departmental definitions simply be pointers to this main definition.

When one is considering knowledge bases a slightly different, though no less dangerous, form of redundancy can occur. Suppose that the system contains a number of rules each of which "tells" the inference engine to try rule 123 next as this is a heuristically wise move. Suppose now that this wise next step is changed, moved or deleted. This means that rule 123 is not the same as it was before. Unfortunately all the other rules still refer to it. This is where problems arise. Other possible areas for redundancy to arise occur when, for example, a list of possible goals or hypothesis is kept separate from the rules to which they occur. It would be easy to add rules without adding goals or to remove rules without removing the corresponding goals.

3.7 Summary

In this chapter we have introduced a number of different methods for representing knowledge about the world. The most common of the forms is the production rule. This was described in some detail together with the methods that the inference engine uses to manipulate production rules. Finally we have related production rules to the other knowledge representations and talked about the important issue of modularity.

Chapter 4

Tools for Developing Expert Systems

4.1 Automated tools to assist in the creation of Expert Systems

If expert systems are to be accepted as a form of computer program to be used in real life situations it will be necessary to provide a large number of working systems in a wide selection of domains. To speed up this process it will be necessary to have tools and methodologies to assist in the creation of the expert systems. The realisation of this fact is only beginning to arrive. (Keller, 1987)

An indication of the problems faced by not using appropriate tools is that the most frequently quoted Expert System (MYCIN) has been abandoned because of difficulties inherent in maintaining the system (Moore, 1987). The reasons for these breakdowns are two fold - firstly they arise because of the lack of tools for development but secondly, and perhaps most importantly, because the lessons of software engineering and the traditional life cycle have been forgotten or ignored in the rush to demonstrate the plausibility of the field.

In this chapter we consider the tools that do exist for creating Expert Systems and we also examine the need for a software engineering approach to be applied to the development of Expert Systems.

In most of the literature the tools described to create Expert Systems are based on those that produce the actual runtime system. Whilst this part of the process is undoubtably important and often affects the knowledge acquisition process by imposing constraints on how the data and knowledge can be stored and manipulated, the important step of knowledge acquisition is still relatively unautomated.

4.2 Knowledge acquisition tools

The most common forms of knowledge acquisition are usually undertaken at the human level - interviews (both structured and unstructured, generalised checklists, group interviews, critical incident techniques, reclassification etc.), questionnaires, multidimensional scaling and protocol analysis - although these may be assisted by computer based tools. For example the transcripts of interviews can be written as text files and sophisticated indexing and keyword searching techniques can be used to isolate the main points that the expert mentions. It is also possible to use computerised tools to examine the amount of time spent using certain pieces of information such as spreadsheets, databases and textfiles. (Hayes, 1987)

Those automated tools that do exist are generally of two types - firstly there are those systems that are essentially "intelligent editors". These are programs that allow the user to enter the rules in a form closer to English than normal thereby aiding the understandability of the knowledge. Secondly there are tools that work by using a set of examples to induce the knowledge that underlies them.

Intelligent Editors

As we have stated earlier, there are considerable benefits to allowing the knowledge engineer to enter the knowledge in a form that the expert can immediately understand. The process used to implement this is, however, often fairly complicated. In most systems or this kind, there are implicit assumptions about the way in which the knowledge is to be stored, most often in rules.

An example of this this type of system is TERIESIAS. This system provides knowledge acquisition facilities for expert systems based on the MYCIN system.

The method used in TERIESIAS is that the user enters a rule (either as a new piece of knowledge, or as a correction to the existing system) and the system then analyses the clauses and shows the expert its interpretation of them (based on certain knowledge that has already been given to the system). If the systems "understanding" (interpretation) of the parts of the rule is not correct, the user asks the system to use its next best interpretation. This process continues until the system comes up with an interpretation that the user agrees with.

A sample interaction with TERIESIAS (Davis, 1979):
(User replies are shown in *italics*).

The new rule will be called RULE383
IF: 1 - The patients infection is primary bacteremia
and 2 - The site is one of the sterile sites
and 3 -
THEN: 1 - There is evidence (.8) that the category is enterobacteriaceae

This may take a few moments ...
(10-30 seconds of CPU time)

... This is my understanding of your rule

RULE383
IF: 1) Primary-bacteremia is an associated infection for which therapy would cover, and
2) The infection with the organism was acquired while the patient was hospitalized and
3) The culture was taken from a sterile source
4) The organism is not normally found at this site
THEN: There is strongly suggestive evidence (.8) that the category of the organism is enterobacteriaceae

Okay ? (Yes or No)
N
Change premise
Y
What clause should be changed in premise ?
(type Help for list of commands)

Change 1
Suppose (1) were changed to read
1 - The infection is primary-bacteremia
would that be okay ?
Y

A different approach, designed for rule based expert systems, is described in (Doukidis & Whitley, 1988). The technique is essentially a sophisticated pattern matching process, in that it allows parts of rules to match other parts of different rules, if they both have the same "meaning" rather than both being exactly the same, character by character.

The technique works by assuming that there is one main action or relation in a statement and that this relation has a number of pieces of information that also need to be specified before the main "meaning" of the sentence can be found. For example *John picked up the pen* has the main action of *picking* and for the full "information content" to be transferred it is also necessary to specify who is doing the picking, and what is being picked up. The sentence therefore is essentially saying *picking John Pen*. If there is another sentence that says, for example, *John was in the process of picking up the pen*, a character by character match would obviously fail, whilst if we apply the same method of relation and parameters, we would again get *picking John Pen*. If the system used this form, the two sentences would match.

An extra level of complexity can be handled when one considers a sentence such as *the ball is red*. At first sight this would appear to have no action or relation (other than the totally ambiguous *is*). If we consider then the sentence *the colour of the ball is red*, we would say that it was equivalent to *the ball is red*. Thus we can see that the word, because it is a colour is implying a relation *colour*.

Induction

The second type of knowledge acquisition tool is that found in systems like EXPERT-EASE and Xi Rule. They are based on Quinlan's ID3 induction algorithm. Induction works by taking a number of example cases, known as the training set, from the problem domain and listing them under a series of different attributes. So, for example, one might list a number of cases for travel expenses under the attributes amount claimed, duration of trip, reason for trip and expenses paid. The algorithm then proceeds by examining the cases and trying to find the rule(s) that govern the decision making process. It is important to note that there is an implicit assumption that there is some method behind the decisions. The algorithm presents the rules based on the cases and highlights any areas where there are contradictions - in one case one decision was made and in an identical case a different decision was made. It can also inform the user if he has not provided enough examples. For example

Attributes			Result
Amount	Duration of trip	Reason for trip	Expenses paid
30	12	Exploratory	100%
120	1	Sales	100%
20	1	Exploratory	100%
60	2	Exploratory	75%

which might produce the rules:

IF amount < 50
THEN paid=100%

IF amount >50
AND Reason = Sales
AND duration < 5 days
THEN Paid = 100%

IF amount >50
AND reason = Exploratory meeting
THEN Paid = 75%
etc.

Problems with induction include the fact that the algorithm can only find the rules if the appropriate attributes are listed. For example, in the travel expenses example shown above, the system would fail to find rules if the actual attribute that mattered was whether or not the claims officer liked the person claiming. Also the algorithm used means that it if the training set is incomplete, rules that would be based on the missing examples are not formulated. For this reason, many firms use induction as a starting point for the knowledge acquisition process and use it to gain the expert's interest in the possibility of using rules to solve the problem before moving onto more sophisticated techniques for the more detailed knowledge.

One other point that needs to be stated is that induction works primarily by correlation, rather than causation, and these two features are not the same. Therefore in some circumstances the system may give a completely wrong rule. Consider a training set which has the attribute of whether a stork nests on a roof and a result of the family in that house being large. The induction algorithm could assume from this data that there is a rule of the form that if there is a stork's nest on the roof then the family will be large. (Storks deliver babies!). The actual (causal) reason for the training set is that a large family, will, in general, have a large house and this house will therefore have a large roof. The large roof is a suitable nest site for the stork.

4.3 Creating a runtime system / System delivery

Assuming that it is possible to overcome the knowledge acquisition process it then becomes necessary to create a runtime system that utilises this information to provide useful information for an end user. The runtime system usually embodies the results of a number of decisions about:

Knowledge storage format
Data storage format
Inference procedure
Conflict resolution
Explanation facility
Matching technique.

The tools to develop expert systems can be viewed on a language-tool continuum (Harmon & King, 1985) (Harmon et al, 1988). We favour a two dimensional approach (see figure 4.1). Note that both axes use a scale from Rapid, through Easy to Flexible.

For knowledge representation Rapid structures are associated with those found in expert systems shells where the user is restricted to using, for example integers and reals. An Easy representation is used when the system offers a wide variety of predefined structures (such as frames and semantic networks) as well as allowing the user to manipulate and improve them with ease. Flexible representation structures are those provided primarily by high level languages whereby the user is able to create any representation he wishes. Whilst there is an argument in favour of using flexible tools for efficiency purposes it is often the case that all prototyping and testing will be done in a system with Easy structures before the system is rewritten in a more efficient flexibly structured tool. For example the DELTA/CATS expert system was originally developed with a LISP based tool, but it was then converted to a FORTH based tool for speed and portability.

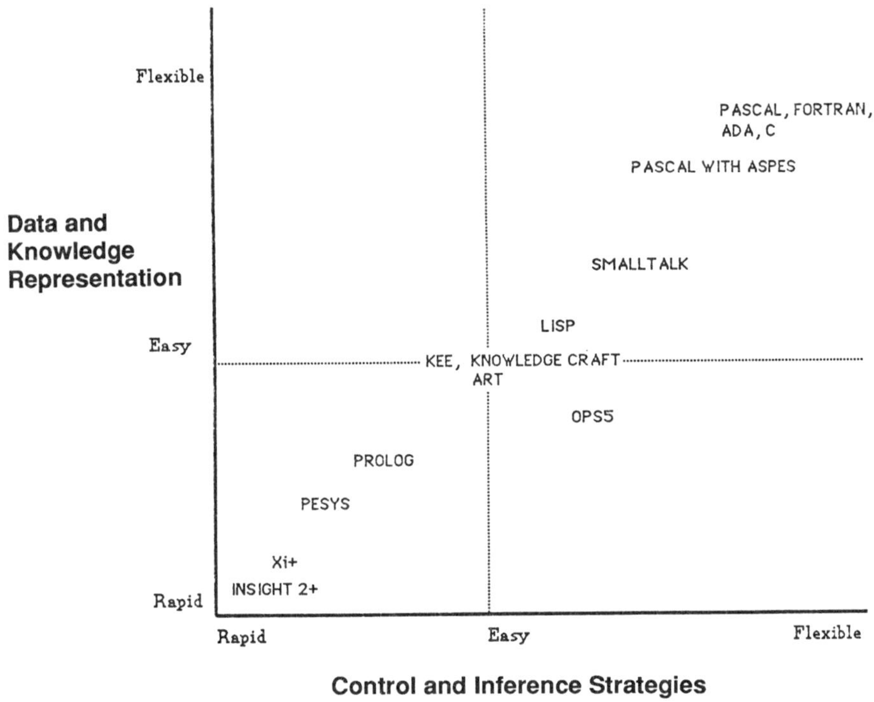

Figure 4.1 System Delivery Tools

Similarly on the inference and control structures, Expert System shells and languages like PROLOG are limited to a few, strictly controlled inference mechanisms which allow rapid system development whilst systems like ORB (Fickas, 1987) and KEE allow easy to use user-defined control strategies.

Again high level languages allow the user full control over the control of inference, at the cost of having to write all the code for himself (although systems like ASPES (Doukidis & Paul, 1987) include prewritten modules if necessary).

4.3.1 Languages

LISP

LISP was developed in the United States by John McCarthy in the late 1950s. It has been the primary language for AI research in the US since that time.

Lisp has one data type, the list - hence the language is known as a LISt Processor. The items of a list can either be lists or atoms. Atoms, in turn, can either be symbolic atoms or numbers. The list (SIZE LARGE) contains two atoms - the symbol SIZE and the symbol LARGE. A more complex list, ((SIZE LARGE) TABLE), contains two items, a list (SIZE LARGE) and a symbol TABLE. Similarly the first item of the list can itself be broken into two atoms SIZE and LARGE.

The language is a threaded-interpretive-language which means that function definitions are based entirely on previously defined function definitions. The base level of LISP is a handful of (badly named) functions like CONS, CAR and CDR. These names (which did mean something in the original version of the language) have unfortunately remained with the language since its inception. The unfriendly terms used in the language add to the considerable problems caused by the nested lists surrounded by parenthesis (brackets) that make up the function. For example

```
(DEFUN DELETE (ITEM LST)
 (COND ((NULL LST) NIL)
    ((EQL (CAR LST) ITEM) (CDR LST))
    (T (CONS (CAR LST) (DELETE ITEM (CDR LST))))))
```

is a simple function to delete an element from a list. This lack of readability of LISP can cause considerable problems if someone other than the original programmer attempts to maintain or modify the code.

Since a LISP system only needs these few primary functions to start with, most actual versions of LISP add a large number of further functions on top of the basic ones. These added functions mean that the support environment for language approach that of a programming environment. The environment is interactive and the debugging facilities allow one to examine the state of the variables at any point of the interaction.

There is (of course) no standard set of functions to be added to a system and therefore there is no standardised version of LISP - each version does certain commands in its own way, and each calls its functions by a different name. Indeed as a result of this many versions of LISP contain files that contain the definitions used in other forms of LISP.

Many problems in Artificial Intelligence are of a recursive nature, and LISP is primarily a recursive language making it an ideal tool to solve these problems.

A large number of data structures such as frames and rules are easily coded in LISP and the manipulation of these structures is also very easy. For example if a system had a production rule in a list one primitive function is needed to access the IF parts (the first element in a list) and one primitive is needed to access the THEN parts (the next element in the list). Since program code and data have the same form, it is possible for the user to have "programs" specified as data. This "procedural attachment" is often used in *active rule* systems. For example

```
((IF
   (FACT 1 IS TRUE)
   (FACT 2 IS TRUE)
   (PROCEDURE 1 RETURNS TRUE)
   (PROCEDURE 2 RETURNS TRUE))
 (THEN
   (FACT 3 IS TRUE)
   (FACT 4 IS TRUE)
   (PROCEDURE 3 CAN BE ACTIVATED)
   (PROCEDURE 4 CAN BE ACTIVATED)))
```

In the above rule the system all the if parts and then parts are simply lists and therefore the system will regard as identical the first IF list (FACT 1 IS

TRUE) and the third (PROCEDURE 1 RETURNS TRUE) when it is manipulating the data structure, however, when it comes to checking the rule, it will be able to differentiate between the two types of list. For a suitable introduction to LISP see Doukidis et al., (1988). Chapter 9 also includes a very brief introduction to Lisp.

PROLOG

PROLOG is a programming language based on first order predicate logic and horn clauses. It is a Franco-British development and has come to be seen as the European rival to the American LISP. Prolog is a declarative language in that the user feeds the system facts in a predicate form and queries. The system then tries to solve those queries by using the declared knowledge. The declarative nature of PROLOG means that the user specifies constraints to the problem rather than specifying how the problem is to be solved.

Due to the clause format that is used in PROLOG, the language has often become associated with knowledge base data bases and with the "intelligent" front ends to systems.

As an example of a PROLOG programming, consider the PROLOG statement *likes(John,Mary)*. This is simply a two place predicate relating *John* and *Mary* with *likes*. Since the system knows nothing more about the predicate than what is stated, this does not mean that *likes(Mary,John)* is also true. *Likes(John,Mary)* could just as easily be *larger_than(5,3)*. If we wanted to show that the ordering of John and Mary made no difference, we would have to add a rule such as, *likes(X,Y) :- likes(Y,X)*. Note the use of upper case variables X,Y. The rule states that any X, likes any Y, if any Y, likes any X.

One of the problems that arises with PROLOG is due to the fact that the method solving the problem is left to the interpreter and so if this is badly written the execution of the PROLOG program will suffer accordingly - particularly the user has no means of controlling the search strategy within the PROLOG database, and he has no means of telling the program when to abandon a search. Another important problem with PROLOG is that it only stores true facts, and it is difficult to use the notion of negation. This means that it is difficult to store information such as A is not B since the system cannot distinguish between facts that are known to be false and facts that are unknown. Doubts have also been raised about the philosophical background to PROLOG in the real world - is it really possible to assume that clearly identifiable individuals (or objects) have clearly defined true or false attributes since disputes will arise between groups whenever "one party gains from assigning truth-values differently from another party" - if it were not for this fact there would never be any disputed legal cases. (Stamper et al, 1987)

Languages specifically designed for production rule systems, such as OPS5

A large number of expert systems use IF-THEN production rules to represent the majority of their knowledge and the tools that exist to manipulate the rules are in one extreme, expert system shells, which tend to use passive rules, whilst in the other extreme there are high level languages which provide, to a greater or lesser extent, user written modules to manipulate active and semi-active rules.

Languages like OPS5 ("Official" Production System version 5) (Brownston et al, 1985) and its derivatives are designed to lie between these two extremes. They provide the facilities of the shell approach (in that they allow the user to write their rules according to a specialised format and leave the inference strategy to the system) whilst they have a number of features more commonly associated with high level languages (such as variable binding and the ability to call user defined modules of code).

An OPS5 program starts with a list of definitions of objects that are to exist in the program. These are defined by literalizing the object. For example

```
(literalize Person
        Name
        Age
        Weight
        Hair_colour
        Hobbies
)
```

When seen in this way the compound object is similar to a frame or record type structure. Since OPS5 was originally developed in LISP there is normally no type fixing in the definition phase. For example age could be either a number or a symbol.

To access elements of an object the prefix operator (^) is placed before the element name. By using this facility actual items of data can be added to the system. For example

(Person ^name John ^Hair_colour Brown)

would add brown hair to the object called John. When these facts are used in a rule, the system can check against the values specified. For example

(Person ^age 21)

when used as a condition will retrieve all the people who have a value of 21 in their age field. In this way the system acts in a similar manner to a relational database.

It is also possible to use variables and bind particular values to them when obtaining information. For example

(Person ^age <age-value> ^hair_colour Brown)

would list all the people in the working memory of the system whose hair colour was brown and would bind their age to the variable age-value in every instance. This bound value of age-value can be used as other conditions in the rule or used as part of the then part of the rule.

The inference engine works by examining all the rules and making up a conflict set of possible rules to fire. These rules will be determined by the values obtained from the conditions of the rules. A sophisticated conflict resolution algorithm is then used to decide which rule to use first. The algorithm is based on the recency of the information that has been used, the most recent items are chosen first. This continues until one rule is left to be fired, which it then is.

OPS5 also includes a number of debugging aids which allow the user to set break points etc. It is also possible to display the working memory of the system, either completely or only those items that match a certain pattern.

Object-Orientated Programming Languages, such as Smalltalk

Object orientated programming (O.O.P.) represents an entirely different viewpoint on the art of programming. Normal programming is based on the idea of an algorithm manipulating data objects, whilst in object orientated programming the algorithms are attached to the objects.

Consider, for example, the statement *3 + 4*. In a standard programming language there would be an algorithm (probably part of a calculation routine) that would take two numbers and add them up. O.O.P. works like this : *3* is an object. In particular it is a number object, part of the class of numbers. The object *3* is passed the message + and the argument *4*. As was stated above, the object contains the algorithm for manipulating its messages. Obviously the object *3* will not contain the algorithm for the message +, but since *3* is part of the class of numbers it can inherit the algorithm from the class of numbers. Since the algorithm for + is attached to the class of numbers all numbers can inherit it. It is of course possible, in certain circumstances, to attach a particular algorithm to a particular number.

High level languages, such as Pascal, C, Fortran, Ada, Algol etc.

Standard high level languages have the advantage over almost all other tools (except, to a limited extent, environments) in that they are usually very well supported and documented, the compilers are usually very efficient and they are in general easily ported between computers. They do not normally require specialised (expensive) hardware. They often have highly developed and sophisticated support environments, debuggers and traces for example, as well as employing proven software design techniques such as modularity, iteration, recursion etc.

They allow the user full flexibility to create the data and knowledge structures required, to customise and make as efficient as possible the control and inference strategies. This flexibility, means, of course, that there is a considerable amount of effort required to create the basic facilities and house keeping routines. Once these preliminary functions have been created it is possible to develop systems fairly rapidly.

High level languages with prewritten modules, such as ASPES.

ASPES (A Skeletal Pascal Expert System) was developed at the London School of Economics as a tool for designing, consulting and experimenting with expert systems. Designed originally as a research tool for operational research, it is now also used as a teaching aid to explain, by example, what expert systems are and how they work.

It is written in Pascal since this is the main medium for teaching programming at the school, though versions of ASPES have been written in LISP, PROLOG, C and FORTRAN. It is a skeletal system that allows users to link in those modules that they need. Since they are able to examine the source code it is possible for them to modify the code and add extra features that are relevant to particular domains. By allowing the users to write their own routines as necessary there is no restriction placed on the developer to force the application problem into the language or representation used in a particular tool.

The architecture of ASPES is shown in figure 4.2 and consists of two levels : the executive level and the library units. Each of the library units consists of declarations, procedures and functions concerned with some aspect of expert systems programming. The units are knowledge base maintenance, inference mechanisms, explanation facility, user interface, external system interface and list manipulation. The executive is a program which consists of the controller, the knowledge-base maintenance tool and the inference engine, to which the user adds his own problem specification using the knowledge-base maintenance tool and the inference engine, to which the user adds his own problem specification using, as necessary, the support provided by the units.

The knowledge base is held in an external text file(s) in the form of if-then rules, possible hypothesis to be proved and facts with opposite meanings. When the system is run the knowledge base resides in the working memory as various forms of linked lists of records. The routines in the knowledge base maintenance unit are responsible for transforming specific parts of the knowledge base (text) into meaningful working memory data structures. They also check that the knowledge base is syntactically correct.

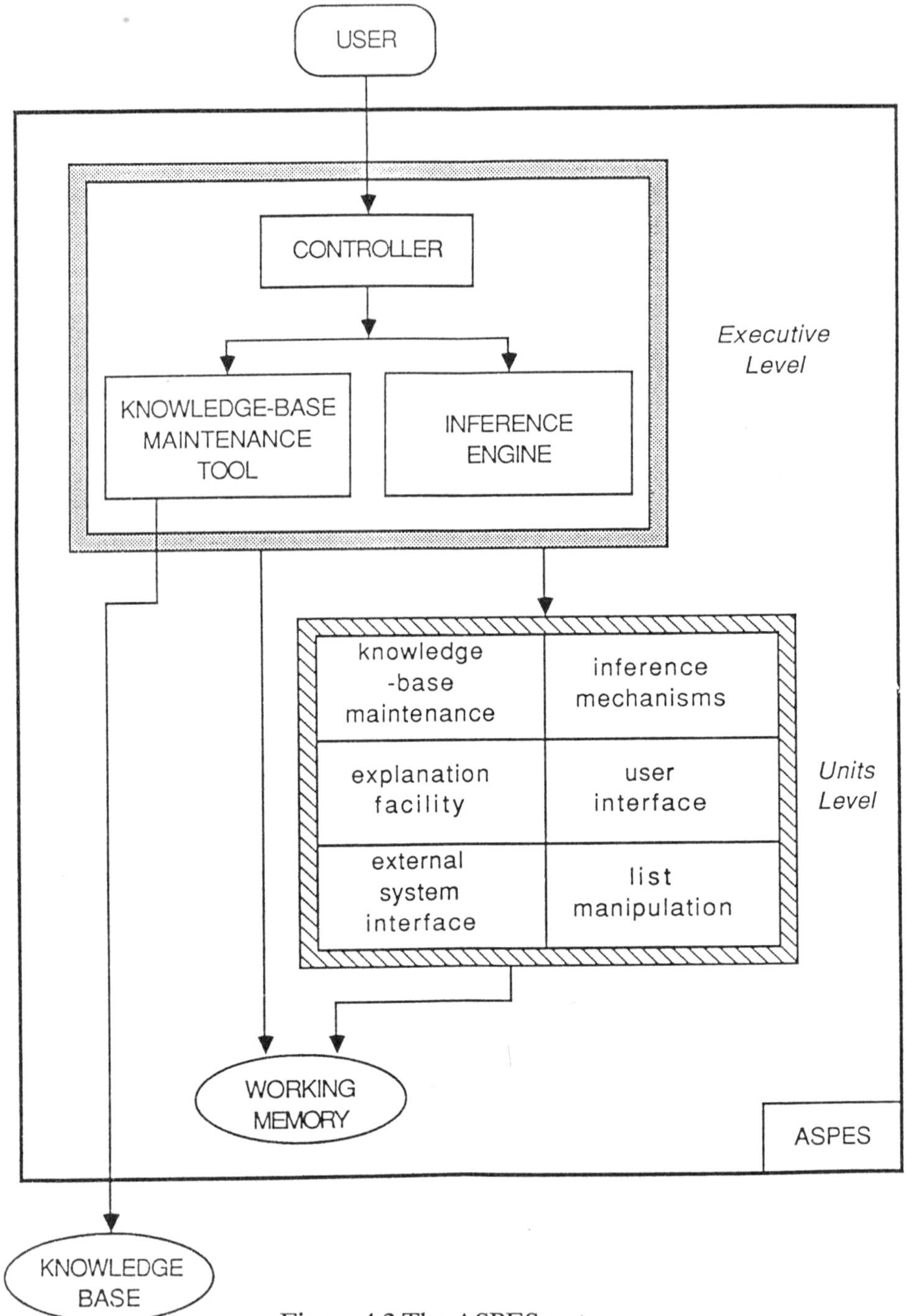

Figure 4.2 The ASPES system

The inference mechanism unit is fundamental as it provides the facilities for chaining and combining the knowledge in a number of different ways. The routines that reside in this unit offer backward chaining, forward chaining or a combination of the two, and they also manipulate part of the working memory by updating the state of the interaction.

The explanation facility unit provides routines for providing the two standard types of explanation. The *why* explanation presents the system's justification for requesting certain information and is provided by tracing the various sub-goals the system is aiming to prove. The *how* explanation shows how the system reached its conclusions during the consultation and is provided by tracing the rule that has just been proved.

The user interface unit provides routines that enable a user to consult with the expert system (but not to construct it). These routines support question answering, menu dialogues and elementary window driven interfaces. The modular nature of the system means that it will be possible to add high resolution screen and pointer facilities quite simply. When the user develops an application (constructs the knowledge base and adds code in the executive) he uses the operating system's editor.

The data structure of the working memory are linked lists of records, and the manipulation unit provides routines for manipulating them (by constructing new lists, updating old lists, returning specific parts or deleting specific parts of lists). This unit is used by most of the other units.

The executive level is the skeletal part of ASPES and consists of three blocks of code : the controller, the knowledge base maintenance tool and the inference engine. The first block is the main coordinator of ASPES and controls the execution, the second block is responsible for converting the various types of knowledge base structures into elements of the working memory, and the third block is responsible for allowing different types of inferencing to be employed.

4.3.2 Expert System Shells

The earliest Expert System Shells were based on existing Expert Systems but simply with the knowledge base removed. This meant that any set of rules that followed the format of the original system could use the shell. The best known example of this approach to shells is EMYCIN which is an empty version of MYCIN. PC based expert system shells, however, have now developed to a stage where they are written from new rather than being versions of existing systems.

Another feature that is becoming more popular is that of the prepackaged Expert System. This is a product that is written with an Expert System Shell, but which comes with a prewritten knowledge base. The idea is that the customer buys an expert system for, for example, the legislation about maternity rights rather than a general expert system. The logical extension to this is that suppliers would sell one copy of the Expert System Shell and then sell a variety of knowledge bases for different areas. The Expert System approach has the obvious advantage that since the knowledge is stored entirely separately from control procedures it is possible to update the knowledge without having to present a new version of the actual program (compare this to, for example, a payroll program which needs to be rewritten every time there are changes in the income tax structure).

Xi+

Xi+ is an expert system shell, developed by Expertech Ltd. a British company based in Slough. It is one of the main products for developing expert systems that is used in the UK. It is also widely used in the United States.

On loading the system the user is presented with a set of four options. He can consult an application, build an application, run the tutorial or exit the system. Expertech also market prewritten knowledge bases for certain domains, such as maternity law, and these systems are consultation only systems, the user is not allowed to build an application.

Within an application it is possible to have a number of different knowledge bases. For example, one could have an application about diagnosing motor faults and have separate knowledge bases for electrical problems, mechanical problems and problems with the fuel supply.

If the user wishes to consult the knowledge base he must select an application. Once that has been done he chooses a particular knowledge base. The next step to be undertaken is to start the query. This option is chosen from a list of available options. Each knowledge base contains a number of queries. By selecting a particular query (or hypothesis) the system tries to prove it using backward chaining.

The rules can contain reports, which are screens of explanatory text, thus the first line of a rule may be a report explaining the purpose of the knowledge base.

When the system is run the user can enter information in a number of different ways. The first method is to select an item from a list.

```
Select one of..
        >> Value1
           Value2
           Value3
  etc.
```

The user moves the cursor (>>) to the appropriate value and presses return. Other attributes may require more than one value, and these are selected in a similar way, however, once all the choices have been made, rather than just one, the user presses the control key and return together to accept the choices. The final method of entering data is simply to type in the value.

Once a consultation is completed, the user has the option to examine the conclusions that have been derived. It is also possible to do a *what if?* type analysis, volunteer data or continue the interaction to see if other conclusions are also found.

Results of interactions can be saved and loaded at any time. It is also possible to obtain information from spreadsheets such as Lotus 123 and databases such as dBase III. It is also possible to load further knowledge bases from within a particular knowledge base, thus aiding the modular breakdown of the system. It is also possible to call up DOS to run other programs etc.

When a user is developing a new knowledge base (possibly within a new application) he can either enter plain text, using the built in editor, or he can edit certain "fields" within the knowledge base. These fields are rules, demons (rules that fire when certain conditions are true independently of the inference strategy), facts that are true - such as numeric constants, questions that are associated with certain facts and a list of queries associated with the knowledge base.

A typical rule in Xi+ looks like

rule 1
if the hotel is class A
  and grade is junior
then outcome is reject

Rules in Xi+ are not assigned names, the system automatically numbers them. Statements can be connected using the logical relation *and* and it is possible to choose between certain values using *or*. For example *if the colour is red or blue ...* . The rules in Xi+ are semi active, in that a form of keyword searching is used. The system splits statements around words like *is*, *are*, *includes* etc. Thus the statement the ball is red, would be split around the word *is* - the ball *is* red. When the system came to query this statement and if the information was not available, the system would ask the user to select the value of *the ball* from a list of all the values that existed to the right of *the ball is* in the knowledge base.

If the system cannot find a keyword in the sentence, it is possible for the user to define his own keywords. The system does not allow the use of the word *not* to specify negations, although it is possible to define the negated forms of the keywords. For example *is not* is the negation of *is*.

A number of documented applications have been produced using Xi+, such as a front end to a nuclear reactor design program, clarifying the law on dismissal and maternity rights (which are available as knowledge bases), dynamic manuals, Tate + Lyle - process plant fault diagnostics and the OKO Bank's Expert System for agricultural loan evaluation.

Insight 2+

Insight 2+ is produced by Level Five Research, a U.S. company. In many ways it is similar to Xi+, although the system also has a number of important differences.

When the system is loaded the user is asked if he wants to Run a knowledge base, Edit one or Compile one. Insight 2+ also offers facilities for the user to manipulate dBase files, using a Turbo Pascal program.

The system allows the user to give their confidence in an answer and therefore one is allowed to set the confidence level for the acceptance of facts. Thus if the confidence THRESHOLD was set to 40, then all facts with a confidence of 40 (out of 100) and above, would be considered true. It is possible to switch the confidence mechanism off.

When writing a new application the user is given a full screen editor and must then write the rules according to certain criteria. The first line of the knowledge base must be the TITLE of the application. (Note that Insight 2+ is particularly fussy in that it requires that all reserved words be written in capitals).

Insight 2+ performs a keyword check (the keyword must be in capitals) in a similar manner to Xi+. However, it also allows the user to specify negations using *not*. If the confidence tests are on the user can be asked to indicate his confidence in the reply by moving a sliding bar.

The Display command is similar to the Xi+ report command. It is also possible to create explain displays. Another facility that is offered by Insight 2+ is the ability to access dBase files. This is done by writing a Turbo Pascal program that manipulates the actual database files. A number of prewritten procedures and functions are available to assist in this task.

4.3.3 - Environments

Environments are currently the most sophisticated form of expert system development tool. Their cost and hardware requirements mean that they are primarily suited to those companies or research establishments that are making a definite effort in the area of expert systems development as opposed to those companies which are simply investigating the area. They also differ from most other tools in that they are not designed simply to have a knowledge base attached, rather they are meant as tools for developing tools. Thus one is more likely to write a shell using an environment and then attach a knowledge base to that newly created shell.

Another feature of environments is that they support many different knowledge representations and inference strategies. Most will contain some form of production rule system, a logic programming and an object orientated programming environment as well as access to LISP and other facilities.

There are very few environments available, and those that are tend to run on very expensive dedicated hardware - in particular the so-called LISP machines such as the Symbolics and TI Explorer, although attempts are being made to port versions of them to top of the range personal computers as well as minicomputers and mainframes. They generally have sophisticated support environments, windowing and graphics facilities in addition to those facilities specifically tailored to expert system creation. The sales of the systems is usually fairly low (less than 500 copies) and the number of (reported) working systems developed is usually small (since the tools are being used as part of a long learning and development process). It is quite probable that the huge cost of developing the systems (especially if the specialist hardware must also be purchased) is not covered in many cases. There is some connection between the list of reported systems in commercial environments and those companies that own equity in the firms producing the environments.

We will now describe the main features of three of the most common systems available - KEE, Knowledge Craft and ART.

KEE

KEE, which is produced by IntelliCorp, is based on object orientated programming, with origins also in INTERLISP. Just as the Apple Macintosh system uses object orientated programming to facilitate its graphic user interface, so KEE uses it to show objects and relationships in its knowledge base.

KEE uses frames as its primary knowledge representation, and it allows these to be linked to rules, logic, data driven reasoning and object orientated programming. In KEE frames are called units and units can be given names and attribute descriptions. It is possible to attach procedures to frames. Both forward and backward chaining are supported and the search strategy used can be either depth or breadth first. Alternatively the user can code his own search strategy. Frames can be represented graphically and the graphics are directly related to the frame values. Thus if a frame contains a slot for temperature then a graphic representation of this may be a thermometer. If the temperature in the slot increases then the mercury level in the thermometer displayed will also increase.

Knowledge Craft

Knowledge Craft is produced by the Carnegie Group and it uses LISP, frames, logic and object-orientated programming. It is based on SRL+ developed by Carnegie Mellon University.

In Knowledge Craft frames are called schemata but functionally they are fairly standard frames. It is possible to place restrictions on slot values.

As well as the main tools in Knowledge Craft, the developer also has an interface to CRL-OPS (which is based on OPS5 and is a forward chaining rule based language) and CRL-PROLOG which is used for backward chaining.

ART

ART, produced by Inference Corporation, is a rule based system based on the OPS5 programming language. It offers frames, logic based programming and LISP for the creation and manipulation of data structures. Facts in the system contain prepositions, for example, A is B and they can also show the extent to which they are true. This is known as logical dependency, since one can state that A is B to whilst C is true. If the truth of C is altered then the truth of A and B will alter accordingly. As an example of this suppose that an expert is making a diagnosis of a system. He assumes that there is a certain fault and based on this, certain other factors will also not be true - if the motor has burnt out, then the internal wheels will not turn. If, however, at some later point, he decides that the motor had not burnt out, then the assumptions that had been made about the internal wheels will also no longer be true. The system can also differentiate between false and unknown information.

The inference strategies in ART are both forward and backward chaining with a blackboard mechanism as its controller.

4.4 The relationship between expert system tools and software engineering

In principle, the Software engineering approach either describes and/or condenses data, whereas the Expert System approach aims at extracting deductions and inferences from a particular set of data related to a specific field. On the other hand, another remarkable characteristic of Software engineering is the efficient storage and retrieval of (sometimes large) quantities of information. Expert System problems, instead, deal with a small amount of information after the system is developed. Large amounts of information are considered only during the development of the Expert System - exactly the opposite of the case in Software Engineering.

In most Software Engineering problems, inference is always related to the quality of the information. Another difference is the kind of information to be dealt with. In Expert Systems we have a set of facts and relationships between them (dynamic information), whereas in Software Engineering we only have the facts (static information). The output of an Expert System is a conclusion based on the information input, used by a deductive mechanism that must be transparent to the user. In S.E., the programmer has, in most cases, an almost complete control of the machine. Therefore, Expert System languages must be, in principle, simple because the designer must be most concerned with the knowledge representation; the simplicity mentioned above is to be understood as similar to the human reasoning. These languages must be as logical and deductive as possible.

4.5 Some problems with developing actual systems and the future requirements of tools

As a piece of software, an expert system is plagued by a number of problems in excess of those likely to be caused by the size of the program. The knowledge bases are subject to rapid revision and modification in view of inconsistencies and incompleteness in the knowledge base. This is further compounded by the fact that the knowledge is often provided by more than one expert. Firstly it has been noted that in most cases adding more people to a problem increases that problem (Brooks, 1982) and secondly there is the fact that when more than one view of a situation is presented, the amount of agreement and acceptance about that situation often falls rapidly.

Another well known problem that occurs in a business situation is that for serious expert system development to receive the go-ahead a prototype must be created and demonstrated. If the prototype is developed using one of the higher level tools described above and only a small section of the problem domain is tackled then a rapid prototype can be developed that suggests an impressive capability for a full system. However, when the full problem is tackled many problems come to light.

The first problem is one of speed - when a system has many hundreds or even thousands of rules to examine, the original system may no longer be able to cope. The final runtime versions of many systems are therefore converted to run on other hardware or in different languages (for example the DELTA system mentioned earlier).

A far more important problem is that of the creation and maintenance of the knowledge base. The Dendral system took over *40* person years to develop. One of the most damning indications of the problems of knowledge base maintenance is given by the MYCIN example. MYCIN was a pioneering Expert System and is still mentioned in almost every paper on expert systems - yet this *400* rule medical diagnosis program, which was developed by a group of doctors who also made themselves into programmers, took *100* person years to develop and was subsequently abandoned since the knowledge was so deeply embedded in the system software that the program was essentially unmaintainable.

Another often mentioned system is the XCON program written by DEC to configure orders for its VAX computers. The results of this are better, but only slightly. It contains *8,000* rules and took *180* person years to develop. This is a *20* fold increase on MYCIN, *but* it takes a 30 person team to maintain it.

A third system, GASOIL, developed by BP to run on VAX machines, is used for the design of offshore hydrocarbon separation equipment. It contains *2,800* rules and was developed part time in about a year. This is another *20* fold increase in productivity, and according to DEC it is the second largest system in the world. The methodology used by BP in its Expert System development means that its maintenance costs are considerably lower than the DEC system. (Moore, 1987)

How will the process of broadening the scope of the development tools proceed? In the automation of conventional systems development a distinction can be made between those approaches that start from the activity of programming, defining it as being the problem, and supporting it as an activity to be structured and controlled, as much as an activity to be automated. This we may loosely term the software engineering approach. In contrast the emerging information engineering school seeks to bypass that activity by automation, and starts its focus far more on the early phases of system development, providing tools that will facilitate communication between users and systems developers, and subsequently generate and regenerate systems throughout their life. The problem is achieving and modifying compatible expressions of specifications, and not just accurately transforming them into code.

In the spirit of the Information Engineering School we have identified twelve general requirements that will need to be addressed by the software environment for expert systems. Many of the requirements are suitable domains for the use of expert systems techniques.

Whilst the requirements appear to follow, in some ways, the classic life cycle model of computer based information systems, it is also clear that knowledge based applications must follow a somewhat different route since large proportions of them are typically under constant revision as their environment changes and knowledge develops. Furthermore the expert system is typically a collaborative venture in which experts, users, knowledge engineers and software engineers must continue to be involved throughout the duration of a system if they are to be successful. The requirements are therefore closely related and not just a list to be checked item by item.

Whilst in the past the tendency has been for expert system designers to look for domains to use their tools with, this is unlikely to be the future trend. It is far more likely that needs will be articulated by users as a result of the analysis of their business problems.

Requirements to be addressed by practical expert system software

- -The determination and subsequent redefinition of requirements
- -Obtaining knowledge
- -Representing knowledge
- -Integrating stored knowledge
- -Integrating and developing the inference system
- -Knowledge maintenance
- -Knowledge portability
- -Security of the knowledge base
- -Validation and Integrity
- -Software maintenance
- -Implementation, Integration and Institutionalisation
- -Interfaces to other software modules.

Once a domain has been identified for the application of expert systems it is necessary to obtain knowledge about the domain. Whilst conventional systems analysis tends to focus on the existing procedures within an organisation, knowledge elicitation tends to focus more on the rules, conventions and norms which underlie the process. The traditional data processing community has become aware of the fact that no one technique can provide more than a flawed model of human activity and behaviour. Some of the newer elicitation methods are likely to meet the same problems, leading to the need to continuously review and validate the state of captured knowledge.

The need to have both computable and understandable forms of knowledge has been discussed in chapter 3. Future systems will probably therefore need to develop the concept of a knowledge dictionary which has the capability of displaying the same knowledge in different representations.

Similarly the knowledge stored in a system will have to be interrogated by both the users and the system. At the present time the interrogation of the knowledge base simply presents the user with a list of facts that have been derived and a trace of how they were derived. There will therefore be a need to allow the system to explain in "greater detail" the information in the knowledge base.

At the current time the inference strategies of expert systems are "simple", being restricted in the most part to forward and backward chaining.

In the future users will wish to use more sophisticated solution methods - dynamic programming, maximum likelihood etc.

As systems grow the problems of maintaining and updating the knowledge base grow too. As was stated earlier the R1/XCON has considerable maintenance problems. One solution proposed is to use more structure in the original knowledge base.

At the present time very little has been done to promote the portability of knowledge between different expert systems. When this problem has been addressed it usually only involves moving from a development environment to a production environment and concentrates more on code than on moving knowledge.

If knowledge bases are built, then they have to be protected. The possibility of "confidential" knowledge being made available to competitors must dictate that security is taken seriously. One must wonder when the first knowledge base theft will emerge, whether it is undertaken by hackers who simply wish to try to "beat" the system or by people deliberately trying to defraud the company.

The integrity of a system encompasses a more general test of the validity of its structure and knowledge base, and is a process that needs to take place continuously. Thus active monitoring of a system is needed throughout its useful life.

Expert systems are software systems, just as any other and will therefore demand maintenance. Experience suggests that expert systems projects start as small scale learning exercises. Once they gain credibility they can become large projects rather fast, and what is more large projects based on loose management concepts such as prototyping, code sharing and reimplementation. This suggests that the provision of tools to aid software maintenance would be extremely valuable for many users.

In the real world, building excellent technology is not enough. It must be introduced and demonstrated in a real application. Expert systems can raise fundamental ethical issues of the role and responsibility of their users, designers and sponsors. Each of whom should demand assurance that they understand and can accept the expert system both as an item of technology in the workplace, and as a shift in the chain of accountability.

Real systems need interfaces to other software modules. A real system must communicate with more than a single user, it must become part of the regular data processing activity of the organisation. For this reason alone we do not foresee a primary role for specialist hardware outside the development environment. Development of expert systems will increasingly be just one part of an ongoing software development portfolio of interlinked projects. The ability of expert systems to inter-work with other software models will become a key requirement.

4.6 Summary

In this chapter we have introduced a number of different tools that can be used to develop expert systems. As is the case with programming, there is no perfect general purpose tool, certain tools are better for certain domains than others. In describing the different types of tools that are available we hope to have assisted the end user in selecting the appropriate tool for their problem.

Once a tool has been selected, it is vitally important that a valid design methodology is followed to implement the system. This is best described if one considers Expert systems as simply a new way of programming (and hence requiring the rules and management of projects etc. that all projects have) rather than some new ideal way of solving any problem without needing to think and plan beforehand. Finally we consider the future market for expert systems.

Chapter 5

Knowledge Acquisition in Practice - A CASE STUDY

5.1 Introduction to the domain

This chapter presents a case study in Knowledge Acquisition (KA). The case study is based on a paper by Poulymenakou & Doukidis written in 1987. It demonstrates a number of techniques that can be used in a knowledge acquisition process, in particular heuristic modelling, critical incident technique and repertory grid, and highlights a number of the problems associated with them.

The case study has two objectives: first, to evaluate more than one knowledge acquisition technique in the context of a real life situation. As Gammack & Young (1985) point out, there is not much significance in looking for "strengths" and "weaknesses" of various KA techniques in order to select the most appropriate ones for a given situation. It is far better to recognise from the beginning that even in a single domain of expertise, the expert's knowledge is of several different kinds. They will demand different KA techniques to capture them efficiently. The second objective is to show how expert system techniques can help the expert understand the domain he is working in and assist him in decision making. This could be accomplished by providing him with a system that constitutes a model of his domain and enables him to store information explicitly. However, it is our belief that the provision of a complete, operating system is not the only way to assist the expert. The whole process of building the system and in particular the KA part, can prove even more helpful than the system itself. KA should not be viewed as a data collection activity. The basic question to be answered here is about the way in which an expert uses his knowledge. This is a two-fold problem: on the one hand, experts are not always aware of the extremely complex information processing mechanism that they utilise when they deal with a problem. Alternatively, their view of the problem is a holistic one; the structure of their knowledge and the intermediate steps they take in problem solving are more often than not unknown to them (Dreyfus & Dreyfus, 1986). During KA the expert gains much insight on these issues, which helps him locate his own needs, his "weak" points. The final outcome of a well conducted KA process, may be that a system is no longer needed.

The expert is a transportation engineer specialised in analysis and development of transportation models. The projects he undertakes are studies of an urban or regional area resulting in the production of a *transport model* (computerised), and a set of *planning proposals*. These will be implemented in optimising planning for transportation development in this area, achieving better management of the existing infrastructure and better programming of investments in the transportation sector. The model is also a tool that can be used in forecasting the impact that future changes in population, income etc. in the area, will have in transportation management and planning. The transportation analyst is involved in all stages of the study from forming the proposal for a transport study, to the final assessment of alternative solutions to transportation problems.

The expert's work as an analyst, begins at the time the consultancy makes a proposal for a transport study. This includes *terms of reference* and a *methodology description* and is prepared by the expert. The document is evaluated by the client and once the project is undertaken, work is partitioned into three major phases with the criteria that an equal amount of time is spent on each of them. The overall aim of transport modelling is to establish relationships between key travel characteristics (pattern, mode, volume, purpose, journey time) activity variables determining travel demand (households, floorspaces, educational attendance) and the networks upon which travel is accommodated. In the first phase of work, the data for the input of the traffic model is accumulated; the analyst reviews existing data to determine what can be used and designs and organises the surveys for the collection of the rest. In the second phase, he develops the traffic model, which is a computerised tool based on a set of mathematical expressions. This set is calibrated to simulate the observed travel characteristics given the appropriate information on the present state of the variables. In the third phase, the output of the model is used to evaluate alternative policy recommendations for transport planning. It must be made clear, however, that the model on its own does not provide recommendations regarding specific projects. Its output are global values that provide the information required for the assessment of planning proposals.

The conclusion of the first discussion with the expert was that a series of activities exist that could serve as "milestones" in the flow of his work due to their importance but also to the fact that they are common to every project. The size and the special demands of each project influence only the complexity that each of the activities will pose during the transport study. The set of the activities is as follows:

-*Selection* of a transport model; the selection is a function of the requested output and the availability of the required data.

-*Identification* of the appropriate data to feed in the model. A selection from the existing data is made and the nature and the amount of the additional data is defined.

-*Estimation* of parameters that the model requires to work.

-*Calibration* of the model.

-*Validation* of the model output.

-*Evaluation* of alternative policy recommendations according to pre-established criteria.

5.2 Heuristic modelling and critical incident technique

There are two different types of issues that one has to consider when one defines a KA strategy for a specific case. Issues of the first type have to do with the selection of a method for proceeding with KA. Issues of the second type, address the problem of selecting one or a number of techniques that will most effectively and efficiently achieve the aims and objectives set by the method. It is the method that defines the "requirements" and the "deliverables" for KA and it is the technique that gets us from the former to the latter. In this case, the method is *heuristic modelling* and the first technique used is the *critical incident*.

5.2.1 The method.

The approach of heuristic modelling is to provide the expert with a set of computer programs that constitute a model of his domain of expertise and enable him to store information explicitly as rules and data. The technique presented by Waterman and Jenkins (1979) aims at building a *heuristic model*, that is an information processing model described in terms of heuristics (rules of thumb) that define its operation.

The primary objective of the method is to help the user of the programs to make complex decisions in an ill defined domain containing large amount of information that must be co-ordinated and used in a short amount of time. Moreover, a framework can be provided within which a high degree of analytic rigour can be imposed. Guidelines for decision-making can be given that structure thinking and direct problem solving. The method is based on three major *assumptions*. The first is that the facts in the domain can be analysed in a formal fashion. The second is that no matter how complex the domain is and how unique the occurring cases, it is anticipated that with a limited number of rules thinking can be guided, the domain can be formalised and analysis of the topic can be enhanced. The third assumption is that the heuristic models of these activities can be formulated as rule-directed models. That signifies the existence of a mapping of the heuristic models on sets of rules that accurately "reflect" them.

The first step in building a heuristic model is formalising the domain. Important decisions that have to be made here include the *selection* of elements of the domain that are relevant to the problem encountered, the way they should be *categorised*, and the pattern that has to be adopted for their *definition*. The data that is collected needs to exhibit such a degree of organisation in order to enable the representation of relationships between the data elements.

The key to formalising the domain is *data extraction*; that is eliciting the knowledge about the domain from an expert. This is accomplished by a series of dialogues between the k-engineer and the expert. The questions aim at revealing assumptions and attitudes that the expert may not have been conscious of. These ideas are then elaborated by both the expert and the KE into a characterisation of the domain.

Rule extraction complements data extraction. The developers of the method maintain that there exists a set of rules that can adequately reflect the above mentioned concepts. Rule extraction again, begins with a set of dialogues. Relevant experience has indicated that the *nature* of the questions asked during these interactions seriously affects the quality of the outcome. By simply requesting, for example: "Tell me all the rules that govern model calibration", very poor results are attained. However, when the expert is asked to present facts within a specified context, for example, "Describe to me the model calibration process in this project" the answers tend to be more clear and specific. So, as is also stated by Waterman & Jenkins, the most successful approach is to focus on particular events and analyse them in great depth.

5.2.2 The technique

In the paper by Waterman & Jenkins the method by which the writers carried out data and rule extraction is hardly presented. The technique we selected to adopt, the *critical incident*, is already known from psychological research (Flanagan, 1954). Flanagan traced with it the important elements that distinguish effective versus ineffective action with regard to a specific task.

The approach here is to focus on memorable events and ask people about their actual experiences at the time. The data collected thus is the most accurate possible as people tend to recall those incidents and they make less mistakes and omissions in describing them. Critical incident techniques will only initiate the process of rule extraction. Its aim is to locate within the different *functions* of expertise the basic *concepts* of the domain. A concept is a key characteristic; it possesses a number of attributes that take certain values. Subsequently, the technique aims at exploring how concepts are linked together to form facts and we think that this is as far as it goes. From there onwards, another technique has to proceed from concepts and facts to the formation of rules. The rules that are generated during the analysis are either specific to a particular context, or a special case that is generally true. We have therefore two types of rules: *axiomatic* ones that are almost always true and *heuristic* ones that have a smaller probability of being true. Both types of rules serve to infer new information but the axiomatic ones are also used to check the validity of the extracted information. Data extraction and rule extraction are two *iterative* processes that progress in parallel. Findings in one provide feedback for the other and both go through numerous cycles before the definition and organisation of relevant data reach a satisfactory degree of accuracy.

5.2.3 Why critical incident technique for heuristic modelling?

It has to be made clear that the KA did not begin with preconceived ideas about how we were going to proceed with it. We expected that the outcome of the first informal discussions would orient us towards the choice of the most appropriate technique. Wielinga & Breuker (1984), state the following as the more severe requirements for the use of a method:

-The amount of acquaintance the KE has with the basic concepts in the domain.

-The amount of co-operation that is required from the expert.

-The amount of interpretation tools to process the data in a consistent way.

We would add to the above list one more factor:

-A preliminary, crude understanding of the expert's knowledge structure.

This includes estimates about the number of different types of problems or functions of the expertise, or of the existing global strategies for problem solving. All of the above issues were evaluated in the preliminary discussions.

In these discussions the first thing to be made sure was that a mutual understanding of what the project was all about was established. The expert was informed about the scope of work and he described to us his work identifying the stages he had to go through to accomplish a given task. Questions like:

-Had you an "instructor" when you made your first steps in the job? or

-If somebody was new in the job, what would be the first task that you would let him complete on his own responsibility?

are aimed at revealing some basic characteristics of the nature of his expertise. For example, if the answer to the first question were positive, this would be an indication that "transferable" parts of his expertise exist. By "transferable" we mean that somebody in the past has been able to describe, transmit, in some way, rules of thumb governing action in the domain. Questions like the second aim at checking whether a hierarchy of importance or difficulty in the flow of activities, decisions or responsibilities exists. Some very useful conclusions included the following:

-Apart from academic experience, his expertise was based upon accumulated experience of everyday practice.

-Experience was gained not so much from dealing with a large number of cases, as from the variety of incidents within a case.

-Decisions about the course of action are highly interrelated with one another. This means that the expert has from the beginning of each case defined how he is going to deal with the whole of it.

At this point, it started becoming obvious that the candidate technique should primarily be a type of *focused* interview. During such a conversation, important issues of the domain of expertise are addressed and discussed but not in great detail. The overall aim is to extract data on the expert's factual knowledge. In the specific case, it seemed that it was not so much the different types of problems but the divergent functions of expertise within a problem situation that were important. So, critical incident was preferred to direct probing about problem types. This technique enables:

-Definition, location and categorisation of all basic concepts in the domain.

It is apparent that the next phase of KA would include:

-In depth analysis of the structure of these concepts and the way they are linked together in reasoning. Explanation of how this influences judgements and decisions.

Therefore, the technique next used should be of the type of *structured* interview, where the questions asked aim at an in depth exploration of the expert's mental model.

Although the applicability of critical incident cannot be theoretically proven, its features satisfied the demands of the case. The basic assumption here is that the domain can be analysed. The first step in analysis, the partitioning of the expert's job into a set of activities, which was achieved in a very early stage, was thought to provide enough assurance that analysis would not lead to a dead end.

5.3 Interviewing: Theory and practice

The nature of the KA process is not usual; it lies in between psychology and cognitive science on the one side and computer science on the other. The technical front of the process is the collection and representation of the data required for the operation of a set of computer programs. However, there is a psychological front to it as well since this data is part of the knowledge of a person. Its extraction requires some sort of human interaction, whose psychological features will seriously affect the quality of the outcome. Therefore, we believe that the first important advantage of the critical incident technique is the fact that since it was first applied in psychological research, it does not underestimate the importance of human interaction. This advantage is further enhanced by the fact that there is no rigid set of rules governing its implementation. It is rather a set of principles which can be modified and adapted to the situation at hand (Flanagan, 1954). Finally, the technique does not have to be used in isolation from any other KA practice; it can be followed up by any other technique suitable for the specific case.

5.3.1 Conditions for a successful interview

Success of the interview is measured by how closely it reached its objectives. In this case, where the objective is information retrieval on a specific subject, success is attaining valid, reliable and precise information. Interviews differ in level of success for a variety of reasons:

-Interviewers differ in skill

-Respondents differ in ability and motivation

-Interview content differs in feasibility

Three factors seem to summarise all the conditions that have to be met in order to achieve a successful interview. Far from being independent, they are rather a set of interrelated conditions. These are *accessibility* of the required data to the respondent; *understanding*, awareness by the respondent of his role and of the information required of him and *motivation* of the respondent to take the role and fulfil its requirements. Accessibility, understanding and motivation apart from being success factors, influence the formulation of interview questions and are used in describing interviewing techniques (Cannel & Kahn, 1968).

5.3.2 Motivation as a condition for the interview

The respondent needs to see that the process of which the interview is a part, is related to his own goals and values. In this case, a conversation was carried out aiming at revealing the expert's attitude towards the whole exercise. The main points of our first discussion, were the following:

-The expert was keen to explore the possibilities that the introduction of an IKBS could open to his job.

-He did declare that he had insufficient knowledge of the subject but he expressed the wish to gain insight and experience on the area of E.S., through this study.

Therefore, there was sufficient motivation initially. Another factor that we regarded as a positive contributor to the expert's motivation is an intrinsic feature of the particular technique that was applied. In critical incident technique the expert is asked to describe a case that he found particularly interesting, difficult, successful, or more than one of these. It is obvious that discussion over such a case could not easily become a boring process. However, the interaction between the respondent and the interviewer also affected the level of motivation of the first. He perceives the behaviour of the interviewer and alters his own accordingly. That is why, for example, it would not be very wise if we expressed our dissatisfaction, disappointment or frustration during an interview, because we were displeased by an intermediate result. This would result in the expert feeling frustrated himself, and later on, when the problem for us would have been cleared up, his frustration could still remain.

5.3.3 Awareness of the respondent of his role

In social psychology, it is very often stressed that the respondent needs to be fully aware of what constitutes completion of his role requirements. He needs to know the terms of reference by which he is being asked to provide data. Without this understanding, it is claimed, data accessible to the respondent is likely to remain unreported. Although this danger was dominant in our case as well, we would argue that defining a role for the expert to fit in could only make things worse. On the contrary, the expert must respond to questions spontaneously so that principles underlying his thought are revealed. For example, when the expert asked : "Would you like me to tell you what parts of my job require expertise ?", we obviously gave him a negative answer. Otherwise, we would risk losing information about what the expert would perceive as being common sense knowledge. This however, could prove to include critical facts about concepts in the domain.

5.3.4 Accessibility of the data

The main problem here does not have to do with the intrinsic content of the material sought. It is rather related to the categories in which the interview requires communication. Problems of language, vocabulary and sophistication are involved. For example, if the expert is requested to clarify an answer where too much technical jargon is involved, he may provide an over-simplified version of it, where important details will be cut off as they are perceived to belong to a higher level of sophistication. In our case, the expert was encouraged to describe things without worrying whether he might become too technical or incomprehensible. Some problems were overcome by the fact that we were familiar with basic concepts in his domain such as mathematical models and statistical functions, that would otherwise require special clarification. However, we also did some introductory reading about his domain, so that we could meet him somewhere half the way in understanding his job.

5.3.5 Interviewing technique

According to Wicks (1984) and Cannell & Kahn (1968), interviewing goes through the following stages:

1.Interview initiation (preparation).
2.Conduct of the interview.
3.Recording of the responses.
4.Analysis of the retrieved information.

In interview *initiation* the interviewer prepares the questions that he is going to ask, plans the structure of the interview, rehearses himself, and even physically "prepares the scene". In this case, we set began by preparing the scene, which was in fact choosing the place that the interviews were going to be held. The choice of the expert's place of work proved very helpful; during our discussion, he was able to demonstrate to us pieces of his work such as reports, charts, etc. We had to prepare no questions and the decisions about the length, the structure and the content of the interviews were straightforward: The meetings with the expert had a predefined duration. As for the structure of the interview, we adopted that of the case that we walked through, maintaining the same partitioning schema.

5.4 Conducting the interview

The aim of critical incident technique was to make the expert describe a case. Theoretically, it was the expert who had to do the talking, however, we had to be prepared to initiate the discussion, e.g. "Tell me; where did you start from?"; encourage him to continue, e.g. "We see"; "yes"; "We understand"; neutrally request additional information e.g.

KE:Who did the data review?
E:We did.
KE:You did; and how did you do it?

or ask him to be more specific, e.g.

E:From previous knowledge, you know what you should avoid and what you should promote.
KE:Could you give me an example within the case?

We tried to minimise possible interruptions, but we realised that listening to the expert without uttering a single word was not beneficial. After a short while he would ask: "Are you with me?". It was more helpful to let him understand that we followed his train of thought. For example:

E:...although you have a shorter time to get the information
KE:...it is bound to be correct.
E:If it is not, you know that isn't .You can...
KE:...check it.
E:... or discard it altogether...

Conversations like those above not only did not interrupt the expert, but also had a relaxing effect after some long, unavoidable monologues.

One aspect we found very interesting, was the use of open and closed questions. In the literature of social psychology nothing is more debated than the issue of "open" versus "closed" questions. Open has to do with the form of the response which a question requires; open questions (also called free-response or unrestricted questions) invite the respondent to reply in his own words. Closed questions (also called restricted or forced-choice questions) ask him to select from a series of alternatives the answer that best approximates the situation. The closed question thus, controls the form, length and content of the possible response. e.g.:

(open) How did you find this formula?
(closed) Did you find this formula by experience or was it written in a text-book?

We used open questions always because they are superior to the closed ones in a number of aspects. Krech (1948) and Cannell & Kahn (1968) maintain that with open questions:

-The way in which the respondent interprets the question is ascertained.

-The level of his information about the subject can be estimated. (We would add that the respondent himself can gain a richer perspective of this subject from these observations).

-Both the structure and the frame of reference for his answer are defined. (We used them for further questioning on the subject).

-The intensity of his feelings on the topic, e.g. its relative importance are revealed.

There have been situations, however, where we did not wish that we analysed a fact to a very high level of detail, which would be at that time disproportionate to the rest of the facts. In the example above, in the first level of analysis we used the closed question.

5.4.1 Recording the data

The amount of information was so large that it was absolutely impossible to avoid the use of a tape recorder. Researchers point out the danger that a recording machine poses, by upsetting the natural flow of the interview and being a constant focus of concern. In practice, both the expert and ourselves very quickly forgot the existence of the tape-recorder. However, the first few questions in the beginning of each interview were deliberately rather irrelevant to the subject of the interview, so that we had time to accustom ourselves to the situation.

5.4.2 Problems with the technique

From the psychological point of view, the technique is both easy to apply and a "friendly" one. The KE and the expert rarely feel oppressed, bored or "stiff" as a result of its application. However, in terms of information retrieval, problems crop up. Critical incident does not take into account *non-verbal* information. Argyle (1973) has particularly emphasised the role of non-verbal communication factors such as: bodily movements, body language, gestures, facial expression, eye movements and eye contact, personal space, proximity, . Moreover, critical incident has the inherent problems of all the other interviewing techniques: (Wielinga & Breuker, 1984)

-Omissions: in recalling some cases the expert may forget to mention many essential features or special conditions.

-Many knowledge states are not accessible for inspection; the knowledge is compiled.

-Knowledge states may prove hard to verbalise, because they require drastic transformations.

None of the above shortcomings can be prevented, however, detection and remedial action are possible. Omissions will be revealed in the analysis of verbal reports and the gaps are going to be filled by subsequent KA. The expert will always respond to some questions by "well, this is experience", or "We don't know, We just do it". By then this mode of questioning will have reached its limits. Although the expert clearly has the knowledge, this cannot be communicated in the interview situation and must be inferred using other techniques.

5.5 Initial knowledge acquisition - Application of the critical incident technique to the case

In applying critical incident, Flanagan (1954), mentions "important events" as he deals with job analysis. Bliss & Ogborn (1979) using the same technique ask their respondents to describe "difficult cases". In this study, we regarded as cases the projects that the expert has completed and as events the activities carried out in the project. Therefore, we first asked the expert to select a case, a project that particularly appealed to him or which he judged to be especially important, or difficult, or both. He chose the last project he was involved in. Then in a series of interviews we walked through it. In the context of this particular case, we focused on all important activities as the expert was asked to give a description of what he did in the framework of each one of them. During the interviews, we were aided by looking at the final report of the project. We were assisted by the presence of the document to visualise the expert's descriptions and understand better what he was explaining. Furthermore, we noticed that it served as a reminder of events for the expert. He was adding elements to his descriptions as he was coming across the relevant notes in the report.

The interviews had the following structure: The expert described a specific activity and as he finished we asked him various questions aiming at:

-Data identification e.g. *"What does an inception report comprise of?"*

-Selection of alternatives for expertise automation e.g.

KE:Is the validation of the data automated?
E:Yes, the computer does it.
KE:Are the checks automatically specified?
E:No, We specify them.

-Establish a chronological hierarchy of decisions e.g. "At what time did you decide the types of surveys you were going to do?"
-Explore interrelations of concepts and decisions e.g.

KE:What made you decide this type of survey?
E:The terms of reference and the configuration of the place.
KE:What elements in the terms of reference did you consider before deciding the type of survey?

5.5.1 Analysis of the data

Analysis of the data constitutes primarily of interpreting the verbal reports that are obtained. The purpose of this process is to establish a mapping between verbal data and knowledge structures. This can be performed at different levels according to the different degrees of depth at which questions about knowledge are asked. The first level of analysis corresponds to the questions asked before and during the critical incident technique. The two aims of this are *knowledge identification* and *knowledge conceptualisation* (Wielinga & Breuker, 1984). In knowledge identification, analysis consists of simply recording what the expert reports of his knowledge. The result is in a formalised form but the representation is based entirely on the way the expert expressed himself. This form makes the review of the data that has been extracted up to this point much easier. We did not create a formal language in terms of fully defining its grammar and syntax. The reason was that this was far too sophisticated a tool for use at this stage. This is an experimental formalisation that is useful as a "reference map". Instead we only used very simple "tools" for the representation of the data:

-Words in CAPITAL letters are terms used by the expert, as they are identified in the transcribed interview. All of them are candidate concepts up to this point.

-Words or expressions in brackets define a type of link or relationship.

-Arrows are used to indicate links or assignments.

For example: "...in defining the input of your model, you have to select the parameters that are easy to forecast, reliable and of a certain validity, however, innovative parameters can be sometimes used."

Formalisation:

```
          (contains)
  MODEL_INPUT------------->PARAMETERS
         (check for) -EASY TO FORECAST
                     -RELIABILITY
                     -VALIDITY
                     -INNOVATIONS
```

In knowledge conceptualisation, the knowledge is formalised in terms of primitive concepts, conceptual relations and conceptual models. Here, the methodology is as follows: from the above formalisation stage, first domain concepts are identified. We classified them under four object types.

Key words: e.g. transport model, enumeration districts, traffic network, roadside interviews.

Procedures: e.g. network definition, review of available data, planning data assembly.

Actions: e.g. sort out data in data review, do traffic counts.

Decisions: e.g. rely on available data, reject a record after range check, take shortcuts from the conventional survey approach. For example:

```
Procedure:REVIEW_OF_AVAILABLE_DATA--->INFORMATION
                (on) DIRECT_OBSERVATIONS
             AND (on) PLANNING_PARAMETERS

Key word:DIRECT_OBSERVATION-->TRAFFIC_COUNT
                   -->TRIP_TIME_ESTIMATE
```

```
Key word:PLANNING_PARAMETER-->EMPLOYMENT
                  -->HOUSING
                  -->FLOORSPACES
                  -->CAR_OWNERSHIP
```

```
Decision:"reject a value after range check" (when)
          VALUE < MIN(RANGE)
       OR VALUE > MAX(RANGE)
      AND Decision:"cannot correct it"
```

Then we look for conceptual relations and here the aim is to trace links among the various concepts in the domain e.g.

```
PLANNING_PARAMETER (affects) DEMOGRAPHIC_PROJECTIONS
     AND (affects) SOCIO-ECONOMIC_PROJECTIONS
```

The next stage in the analysis is aimed at defining conceptual models. That is uncovering strategies of, for example, what actions to perform under what conditions. Here, we looked for strategic statements:

-"Available data coming from direct observations is of limited value because it is taken by different people, at a different time, when the pattern of development was different".

-"We didn't do any household surveys because there was no national census, no enumeration districts. We would have to do it myself and the resources were not available".

-"There is no way you can go back and collect more data: if you find that you haven't collected enough data to build your model, you've had it. You can pack up and go home".

5.5.2 Outcome and comments

The final question to be answered in order to complete this phase of KA, is where has it brought us. In terms of being acquainted with the expert's domain, the task has been completed. Our comment here is that in practice transport modelling has a lot of differences from the process that the textbooks describe. So, gaining insight in the domain of expertise was not aided by reading in advance. The expert gave us an explanation for this; major advancements in the theory have changed practice in the domain over the past few years. Updated information is found in papers published on specific subjects, in various conferences etc. Moreover, every expert in the domain has developed his own methodology and considerable differences in problem solving strategies are frequent.

In what concerns data extraction, the results were two lists:one consisted of brief definitions of terms which we used as a guide in all subsequent interviews. We also used the terms as "poles" around which we asked the questions in the focused interview. The second list gave, in chronological order, the activities and the main procedures in each of them. It was something like a road-map indicating only big cities and main roads connecting them.

The outcome of the application of the critical incident had various facets. First, in the presence of the case we verified all the above results. The formation of the concepts compared to the "road-map" gave us the first comprehensive flavour of what was going on. The combination of those two revealed the main "gaps" in our information; there certainly was no lack of concepts, however, there seemed to be still a long way to go in order to reach the rule level. The links between concepts were few, ill-defined and scattered. The technique is very useful in providing a list of important issues in the domain, only in what concerns fragmented pieces of information. Important links of them were not part of the outcome. Therefore, we knew that we had to proceed with a technique that would have its strong point, exactly where critical incident's weakness was situated. Repertory grid (Hart, 1986) seemed a reasonable choice. It is a relationship-producing technique that can be implemented based on a minimum set of assumptions.

5.6 Further knowledge acquisition: The repertory grid

Once the initial knowledge about the domain has been elicited, it is necessary to obtain deeper knowledge. This deeper knowledge involves finding the underlying causal links between items, finding items in the domain that are similar to one another etc.

5.6.1 The technique

The theory of the technique is based on a model of human thinking, the *personal construct theory*, developed by Kelly (1955). According to it, each individual is a scientist with his own personal model of the world. The aim of it is to predict and control events by forming theories, testing hypotheses and weighing experimental evidence. This model could be used as a view of the expert at work. Elicitation of it could provide a description of how it has developed and how he uses his knowledge. The repertory grid is actually an illustration of the expert's view in a particular problem. A grid constitutes of *constructs* and *elements*. A construct is a bipolar characteristic that each of the elements has to some extent. So, the grid is finally a table of values of elements against constructs; it is a cross-referencing system between them. The technique stems from the methodology Kelly himself has developed for his clients. He applied the repertory grid test for extracting role models: he asked his clients to list, compare and rate role models to derive and analyse character traits. Elements of these models were then used to built a rating grid, which was analysed with a non parametric analysis method (Kelly, 1963). The results helped Kelly and the client to understand the degree of similarity between traits. He named the trait and its opposite a construct and hypothesised that each construct represented some internal concept for the client. Kelly's beliefs of the organisation and use of these constructs, constituted personal construct theory.

In KA elements and constructs have to be elicited. As the expert selects the constructs he must understand what makes a valid construct and how it is used. Each element is rated according to each construct using a subjective rating supplied by the expert. He can describe his ratings by names if he finds that easier, but the most usual is to use a numerical scale e.g. from 1 to 5, which must be the same throughout all the cases. This rating enables elements to be ranked or compared. The elements are in fact key examples produced by the expert and described by the values of the constructs. Once the grid has been elicited, it can be analysed. Methods of analysis include factor analysis and principal component analysis. Shaw (1981), has used a simple method : *cluster analysis*. Here elements and constructs (objects) are compared and a measure of difference between two objects is defined. Objects are then grouped into clusters; those in the same cluster are more similar than those in different clusters. The results of the grid analysis enable attributes and elements to be ordered so that similar objects appear next to each other in a focused grid.

The method has benefits for both the K.E. and the expert. The first, from the focused grid will derive the following:

-Relationships between objects.

-Patterns or associations of elements in the case. They will normally be at a conceptual level and they can be used for further investigation.

For the expert the elicitation of the grid could:

-Make him think twice about a problem; he is helped to clarify issues in his mind.

-Make him get a better idea of rules , i.e. his perception may become clearer.

-Give him alternatives as to how to subdivide a complex problem into smaller ones.

5.6.2 Justification of the choice

The main objection to the method, is we believe its strongest point for this specific case. Owing to the nature of the theory, the results of the method are judged to be very personal, that is very subjective. However, as was mentioned earlier, the way that experts deal with the kind of problems we examined is very subjective. After all, as Newell & Simon (1972) point out, it is the way in which experts see problems that distinguishes them from novices. Another reason for selecting this technique was that after the application of critical incident technique, we found that the knowledge elicited was a big set of pieces of information that could not be exploited and hence formalised unless relationships and structures among them were better defined. The grid was also a good way of judging the validity to the data that we had so far collected; it was reasonable to expect that the grid's constructs coincide with some of the concepts already elicited.

5.6.3 Application of the technique: Grid elicitation

As we have already mentioned, the expert's work is formally divided into three phases. Data review and collection is the first of them and the one we chose to apply the repertory grid. We had to use a subset of the whole domain because the number of concepts indicated that a grid drawn from all the case would be too large and hence quite unmanageable. In the first phase of his work, the expert has, in general terms, to define the data that constitute the input of his model. If the data exists he has to decide on what and how much of it he is going to use. The rest has to be collected through three types of surveys: Household interviews, roadside interviews and traffic counts. He has to decide both the type and the content of the configuration of surveys that he is going to use in each case. The elements of the grid were the projects that the expert had completed to the point. We had five elements and the next task was the elicitation of the constructs. Using the same method as Hart (1986), we chose (at random) a triad of elements and asked:

"Consider cases A, B and C . Can you tell me in what way two are similar and different from the third ?".

The aim of the question is in general to identify a construct (similarity) and its poles (difference). However, the answer in this case was:

E: "They have nothing in common".
KE: "Let's take another triad; B, C and D. What about them?".
E: "No, everything was different".

Then we thought of using one of the concepts elicited in the previous phase:

KE: "In the study we examined, you adopted an unconventional approach for the surveys. Can you point at another case you did that" ?
E: "No, you see there are cases where we did no surveys".

We went back to the previous kind of questions:

KE: "You said that you cannot compare your projects because everything was different. Can you tell me why" ?
E: "You see, the data you find in each place is different in terms of accuracy, size, availability, age...".
KE: "OK. Can you rank the data according to their age for each case" ?

E: "Yes".

So, we got started. Once the expert had understood what were the requirements of the technique, we had no difficulty. In this method, it is easy for the expert to correct his own omissions, by adding constructs where needed. We ranked the elements against the constructs from 1 to 5.

5.6.4 Analysis of the data

Once the grid has been elicited, in order to perform clustering on the elements or constructs, the method used was cluster analysis. To do that, a way of measuring the difference has to be defined. For elements, the measure used was the sum of the absolute values of the differences between ratings. Then their similarity can be calculated.

For the table of similarities of constructs we needed to compare reversed constructs as well as constructs. The measure of similarity was: S(we, j) = 100 -(200*D(we, j))/52.

From the tables of similarities, we can draw the two clusterings . The above calculations were not difficult, however they were time consuming. A pascal program was designed that takes as input the grid and produces the two similarity tables that follow. Automating the calculations has also the advantage that constructs or elements can be easily added or the whole procedure can be applied for the next phase of the expert's work.

The aim of cluster analysis is to reveal which construct (or element) is similar to what and how similar it is. This will then provide links and relations between constructs. In this case for example, the clustering has shown that constructs C1 and C4 (age of available data and validity of them) are very closely related, they have 90% similarity. From this, it can be inferred, that the older the data is, the less valid it becomes.

The results of the analysis are shown in figure 5.1, 5.2 and 5.3.

The following list gives 13 constructs that were found in the domain and for each of them the two poles of ranking are given and the values for five different projects (A-E) are given.

C1 : Age of data available
10 years old = 1
recent = 5

C2 : Size of pre-existing studies
Preliminary evaluation of network = 1
simplified study = 3
fully fledged study = 5

C3 : Degree of network development
Low change = 1
High change = 5

C4 : Validity of available data
Low = 1
High = 5

C5 : Household interviews (sample size)
0 % = 1
5 % = 5

C6 : Household interviews (number of households)
0 = 1
4000 = 5

C7 : Household interviews (No of questions)
No questions = 1
Only travel characteristics = 3
Socio-Economic + travel ch. = 5

C8 : Roadside interviews
0 stations = 1
23 stations = 5

C9 : Number of traffic counts
0 = 1
100 = 5

C10 : Terms of reference (time scale)

10 years = 1
40 years = 5

C11 : Terms of reference (modes)

All = 5
Bus and road = 3
Road only = 1

C12 : Terms of reference (economic evaluation)

Nothing = 1
Costing only = 3
Full scale = 5

C13 : Terms of reference (overall demand)

Low = 1
High = 5

<u>The ranking of the five projects agains the 13 constructs</u>

	A	B	C	D	E
C1 -	3	5	1	3	3
C2 -	3	5	1	5	3
c3 -	3	4	1	2	5
c4 -	2	5	1	3	3
c5 -	5	1	5	2	1
c6 -	5	1	5	3	1
c7 -	3	1	5	5	1
c8 -	2	1	2	5	4
c9 -	4	1	3	4	5
c10 -	1	5	2	2	3
c11 -	1	4	3	5	1
c12 -	1	3	2	5	4
c13 -	1	3	3	5	3

Figure 5.1 The attributes of the domain and their rankings.

The clusters of the cases :

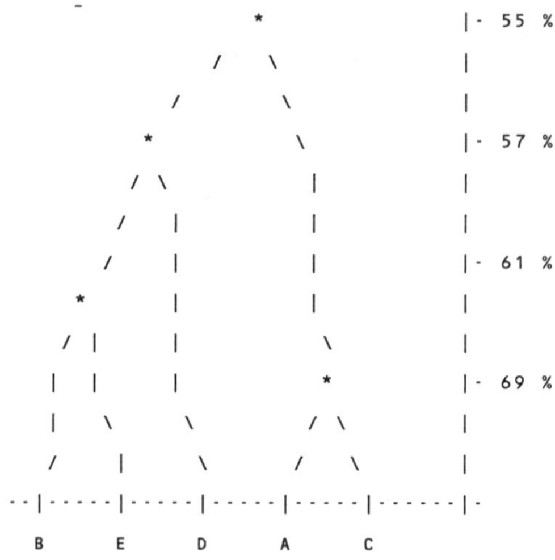

Figure 5.2 The clusters of cases

The clusters of constructs:

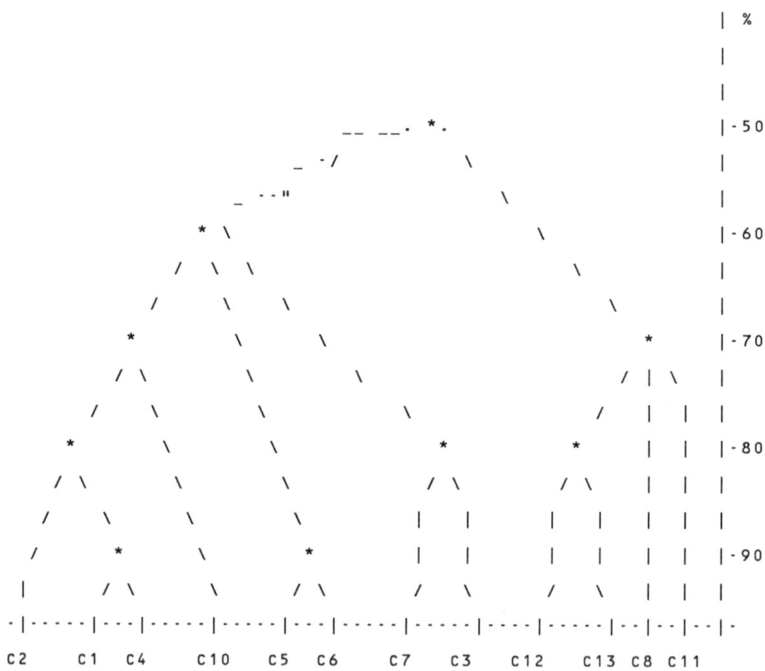

Figure 5.3 The cluster of constructs

5.7 Concluding remarks

"Now you made me think of all these things we have never thought before". The statement was made by the expert. We believe that it contains most of the meaning of the work that is done here. The expert is helped to structure the problem-solving knowledge based on his own operative internal construct network. The point of this exercise was to reveal the construct relations. The only suggested future work is that the expert examines the clustering, and the relations derived by the method. Both ambiguous relations and relations with which the expert disagrees are important points of conflict in the expert's problem solving methods.

The analysis however, does not intend to make the expert change his mind. The feedback from the grid will be the initiation point for further exploration of his mental model. An interviewing phase will aim at expanding and verifying the relationships pointed out by the grid analysis.

5.8 Summary

This chapter has described a number of important methods for use in knowledge acquisition. It also demonstrates that the description of the methods is often based on "ideal conditions". In many cases the knowledge engineer must use his initiative to overcome problems that the method did not foresee, such as the inability of the expert to find similar and different items in the triads. This shows the importance of the knowledge engineer understanding the implicit methodology underlying the technique so that certain steps can be skipped. For example, repertory grid is based on ranking items according to attributes, and one possible way of doing this is to compare items in triads.

Chapter 6

The PESYS System

6.1 Introduction to PESYS

The PESYS system was first described in a paper by Doukidis & Whitley (1988) and the following chapters describe the new version of the system in more detail.

6.1.1 Aims and Philosophy

An Expert System Shell is a software tool that provides the user with certain key features to enable the rapid development of expert systems by the addition, usually, of only the knowledge base. The features highlighted by PESYS are the following : a ready made inference engine, knowledge representation structures, an interface for users and, most importantly, an implicit development methodology. They are designed with the intention to be used by the less experienced users and make possible rapid system development.

Current expert system shells have a number of problems. Firstly the knowledge bases are often difficult to create - having awkward syntax and semantic rules. They are often not very easy to read and hence are difficult to debug. These problems mean that in many cases it is necessary for an experienced user to be employed who will be able to convert the knowledge of the expert into the precise format that the expert system requires.

For these reasons one main philosophy behind the PESYS system was for the rules and all related information to be defined in a form as close to natural language as is possible. This approach has a number of advantages - often it is possible to copy existing rules from official sources and use them directly in the system and if errors such as inconsistencies or missing rules do occur in the knowledge base, it will be easy for the user to spot them, because the rules are so easy to understand, thus making debugging a relatively easy process. It also means that experts can understand the knowledge contained in the rules and they are then more likely to be prepared to accept responsibility for it.

6.1.2 An overview of the problems with existing expert system shells and development tools

Expert system shells and particularly those implemented on personal computers have a number of limitations - although these are being overcome. Here we discuss only those that have been addressed by PESYS. Others include the size of the knowledge base, the rigid structure of knowledge representation techniques and inference procedures.

The interface with the user has developed considerably since the simple typing of *Yes* or *No*. Almost all systems now use menus and offer the users a choice of legal values. With the development of WIMP (Window, Icon, Mouse, Pull-down-menu) environments this area is improving further. The ultimate aim is to have an intelligent interface that understands the actions and intentions of the user without restricting his to a defined set of commands.

If one is using an induction algorithm, the very nature of the algorithm means that it is not possible for this to be done in a natural language way. In systems where the knowledge is entered in rule format - the earliest examples were in LISP - the process was again not done in a natural language way.

```
(RULE IDENTIFY 5
    (IF ((> ANIMAL) EATS MEAT))
    (THEN ((< ANIMAL) IS CARNIVORE)))
```

has an "English" form:

IF the animal eats meat
THEN the animal is carnivore (Winston, 1984)

RULE 085
PREMISE ($AND (SAME CNTXT STAIN GRANMEG)
(SAME CNTXT MORPH ROD)
(SAME CNTXT COMPROM T))
ACTION (CONCLUDE CNTXT IDENT PSEUDOMONAS TALLY .6)

This is a rule that was used in MYCIN and it has the "English" form:

IF 1) The stain of organism is granmeg and
2) The morphology of organism is rod and
3) Patient is a compromised host
THEN There is suggestive evidence (.6) that the identity of the organism is pseudomonas (Shortliffe, 1984)

When compiling the knowledge base the expert (or more likely the knowledge engineer) would have to convert the "English" rules into a system specified format. Whilst this may have been acceptable in the 1960s and 1970s, in the present climate of user friendliness this is not the most desirable approach to use.

PESYS is considerably more user friendly in that it allows the clauses to consist of lines of text. In the current version there is a restriction in that for two lines to match, they must be identical : *It is raining* will not match with *Its raining*. This is, however, a small price to pay for increased readability.

The other main philosophy behind PESYS stems from the original theory of expert systems that stated that the power of the Expert System stemmed from the fact that its rules were kept entirely independent of each other and of the inference engine. In modern systems, especially PC based ones, this fundamental theoretical point is often ignored.

As is described below, PESYS has no information (other than input/output) that is kept separate from the rules - there is no means by which the rules can become dependent on one another, or by which the inference process can be altered by rules - except for when they are fired.

6.2 Consulting an existing application in PESYS

Figure 6.1 presents an overview of the programs used in the PESYS system. As can be seen from the diagram the system can be divided into two sections, the part associated with the development of the knowledge base and the part used for consulting an existing knowledge base.

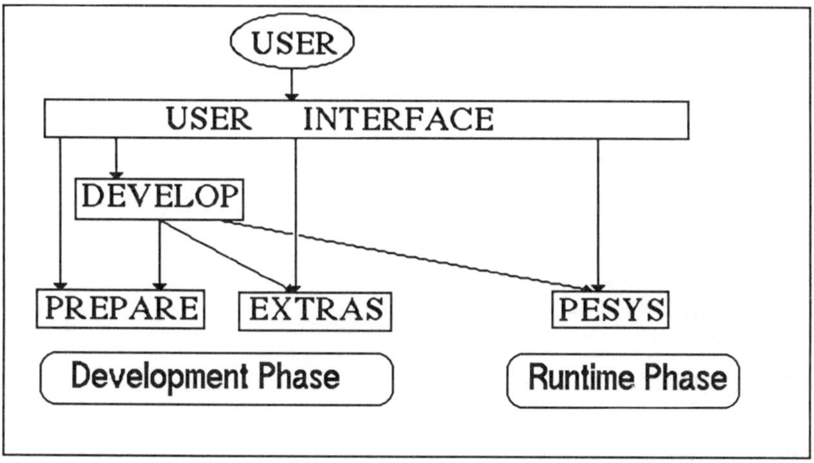

Figure 6.1 How PESYS is structured

Consulting the knowledge base is done through the program PESYS and it can either be called from the Develop program if the developer wants to test a knowledge base, or alternatively - and this is the method used if the user is only consulting the knowledge base - from the system prompt. Once the name of the files has been obtained the system shows a window in which it lists all the files being read. The screen then clears and the user is given the option to alter the configuration of the system (see the section on configuration). Once this has been done the system will probably start asking the user questions.

6.2.1 Answering questions

Yes - No questions

These questions are of the form :

Is it the case that
xxx xxx xxx xxx

Yes *No* *Unknown Explain Prompt*

If there are no prompts available for this question then the system will show the following choices :

Yes *No Unknown Explain*

The user then uses the select menu to choose which is appropriate. Select *Yes* if the statement xxx xxx xxx xxx is true, select *No* if the statement xxx xxx xxx xxx is false, select *Unknown* if the user is unsure about the statement, select *Explain* for an explanation of How and Why this question is being asked and finally, if it is available, select *Prompt* for a prompt.

If a prompt has been displayed the user must press any key to continue.

The explanation facility is explained in more detail below.

Enter a value questions

These are simply questions where the user is asked to enter a value, the type of answer required is usually described in the question given. Note that if the question is asking for a number and text is entered, a value of 0 is used.

At any time during inferencing the system may display inform statements on the screen, these are shown until the user presses a key.

6.2.2 Using the selection menus

Whenever the program wants the user to select an option or value from a list the user makes a "selection". Making a selection involves moving a selector (a selector is shown on the screen by being a different colour) to the value that is required.

The selector can be moved around the screen by using the cursor keys. The selector can be moved around all the available options. As the right cursor key is pressed all the available choices will be shown. The left key moves the cursor back to the previous choice. The up and down keys will move up and down the screen (if that is possible). The space key also moves the cursor right.

In most of the selection menus in PESYS pressing the escape key (marked ESC) will bring up the configuration menu, allowing the user to alter the system as it is run (the configuration menu is described in a separate section). If the Return or Enter keys are pressed the item that is shown by the selector at that time will be "selected".

6.2.3 The Explanation facility

A lot of the power of expert systems comes from their ability to explain their reasoning. This is particularly the case in PESYS since the system uses natural language rule clauses and meaningful rule names.

When the explanation facility is called the system is currently trying to prove a certain clause within a particular rule. The clause being asked and the rule it is from are displayed on the screen as well as the particular clause that the rule is being used to prove.

The sets of OR clauses and ATLEAST clauses (see chapter 7 for an explanation of these) are surrounded by curly ({ }) brackets to distinguish them from other clauses. At the start of each if clause line there is a symbol. Each symbol specifies a different type of clause.

- This symbol means that the clause is a command and as such is always true

? This symbol means that the clause is an ordinary clause and its value is unknown

✓ This symbol means that the clause is an ordinary clause that is known to be true.

X This symbol means that the clause is an ordinary clause and it is known to be false.

The user then has three options. He can return to the previous level, this is either the previous explanation, or back to the question selection.

Alternatively he can ask how a particular clause was chosen. Note that only those clauses that have already been proven (true or false) can be explained and they are numbered. If there are no proven clauses then the user will be told of this fact. If there is only one proven clause then this is selected for explaining how it was proven otherwise the user is asked to enter the number corresponding to the clause to explained. The final explanation is to ask why this question was being asked.

Once the program has finished running, the user is told of the conclusions that have been proven (or told that no conclusion was derived if this is the case) and given a choice of options. He can choose to have an explanation of how the conclusion was proven, he can print the log of interactions that has been recorded to disk, run a what if analysis to explore different variations of the model, he can run the program again or he can leave the program.

6.3 Developing an application

The development phase (see figure 6.1) consists of three stages. The first stage is the writing of the rules in the rule file (.rul). The second and third stages can either be run from the prompt or using the program Develop.

6.3.1 The program DEVELOP

The program Develop is the front end of the development process and it allows the user to pass through the development process indicating exactly what files are ready and still need to be prepared before the next stage can be run. It is called from the system prompt by typing Develop.

If necessary the main file name can be added after the program otherwise the system will ask for the main file name. A screen will then be drawn indicating which of the files exist. A file that exists has a tick (✓) in front of it and a file that doesn't exist has a cross (X) in front of it. It is possible to chose the program to be run by using the selection menu to move between the three programs. The programs are then selected by pressing return. If the files required for a particular stage are not ready yet, the system will inform the user of this and continue. To exit from the program press Escape.

6.3.2 The program PREPARE

This program can either be called from the system prompt (simply by typing its name with the optional main file name) or from within the Develop program.

Either way the user will be shown the initial configuration menu - an explanation of the questions and what their values do, is given in the section about configuration.

For the True/False questions use the selection menu to select the appropriate answer. When the user is asked for numeric values, pressing return uses the default values.

Once all the configuration questions have been answered the system sets about converting all the rules into a form for the other programs. As this is done the system keeps track of the number of rules so far processed and displays this on screen.

When the program has finished the user is either returned to the system prompt or the Develop program, depending on where the program was called from.

6.3.3 The program EXTRAS

The aim of this program is to interact with the user to provide the extra information that the system needs to run. This information takes two forms - firstly it is the actual text for the prompts and secondly it is the information telling the system where to look to for the values of variables.

Prompt information

When the system comes across a prompt in the rules, it finds the prompt name and asks the user to enter the text associated with that prompt name.

Variable information

The system needs to pieces of information. Firstly it needs to know where the information is to be obtained from - either from the user via the keyboard or from a disk file. This is chosen by using a selection menu. If the information is being taken from the user the system needs to know what the prompting question that will be asked of the user when the value is requested will be. Alternatively if the information is being read from a file then the file name must be specified. If the variable is numeric, the user can also specify the number of decimal places to be used when the variable is displayed (ie independently of the number of decimal places in the system) and he can also specify a valid range for the number. If the number is outside this range, the user is informed of the correct range and must try again.

6.4 The files in PESYS

6.4.1 The filename structure for PESYS

The knowledge base in PESYS is stored in a number of files. Each of these files has a common "main" name and a different three letter extension after this main name to indicate what it contains. Figure 6.2 shows the relationship between each of the files and which program creates each.

.RUL - this is the original file that contains the rules. This is the only file that must be written by the user.

.RLC - this file contains the rules in a coded format suitable for use with the other programs and is created with the program Prepare.

.SNS - this file contains the common sense information used by the system. In this version of PESYS this is only the information telling the system where to read data from - either the keyboard or a disk file. This information is derived with the program Extras.

.CFG - this file contains the start up defaults for the system - inference engine and others. It is created with the program Prepare.

.PRO - this file contains the prompts associated with the queries the system asks. It is created with the program Extras.

.LOG - this is the log file and it stores all the output of the system as it

derives a conclusion. It is a permanent record of the systems activities. It can be printed from within the program, after running the system or used in reports etc.

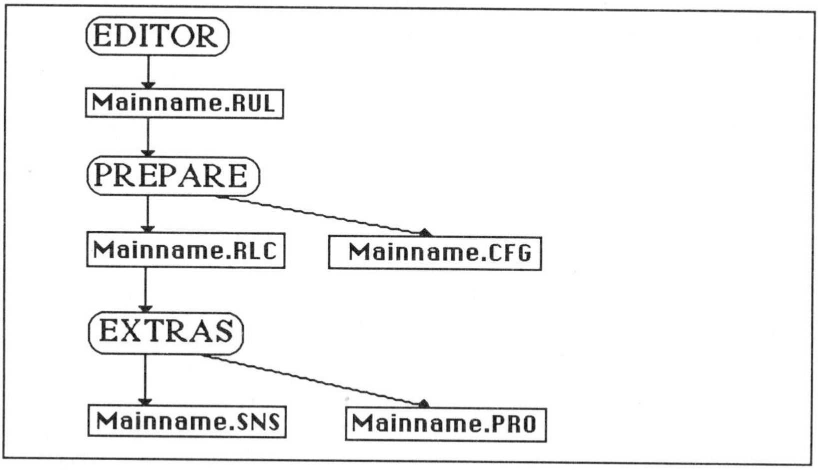

Figure 6.2 The files and the programs in PESYS

6.4.2 Passing the main file name to the applications programs

Each program uses the main file name (to identify the files to be used) and this name can be specified in two ways. Firstly the name can be passed to the program when the program is called. This is done by specifying the file name after the program name when the program is first loaded. For example :

A>PESYS ANIMALS
Main file name

Alternatively if the name is not specified when the program is loaded eg:

A>PESYS

the system then asks the user for the filename.

6.5 Summary

This chapter has introduced the PESYS system. It has shown the user how to answer the questions that the asks in order to prove a conclusion. It has also given a description of the explanation facility. Finally the files used in PESYS have been described.

Chapter 7

Further Details about PESYS

7.1 Configuring the Inference Engine

The inference engine in PESYS is user defined (so that the independence of the rules can be maintained). The configuration that will be used by default for a knowledge base are entered using the program Prepare. The system allows the user to alter the configuration when the program loads or alternatively the configuration can be altered during most of the selection menus by pressing escape.

The configuration menu in Prepare is arranged slightly differently to that in PESYS although the actual information is exactly the same. The menu that is obtained at the start of PESYS and when the Escape key is pressed during the runtime of PESYS will now be explained and then each of the options will be discussed.

The menu shown is

Inference Engine File Operations Other Facilities

If the user selects either Inference Engine or Other Facilities then it is possible to alter the configuration data. The File Operations are described below.

Forward Chaining

If this is set to true the system will do a forward chain at the start of the inference mechanism. Thus if the user only wants forward chaining for the knowledge base this is set to true and all the others to false. The forward chaining continues until either nothing more can be proven or the system proves an inform level 1 clause (see below for a description of inform clauses etc.). By default this option is set to true.

Backward Chaining

If this is set to true the system starts using backward chaining to try and prove each of the inform level 1 clauses. It continues until either all the inform level 1 clauses have been tried unsuccessfully or a level 1 clause has been proven. By default it is set to true.

Mixed Chaining

In many cases the system can made to appear more intelligent (ie not ask silly questions) by combining forward chaining with backward chaining. This means that rules that are not directly in the line of inference can be fired if their if parts are true. Some Expert System shells give this facility the name Demon. By default it is set to true.

Pure Forward Chaining

The only problem with forward chaining is that there must be some data in the system before any more data can be found (since a rule will only fire if its if parts are true). Pure forward chaining partly overcomes this problem by allowing the system to evaluate commands like Enter etc. This means that some data can be fed into the system to start the inference mechanism off. This should only really be set to true if there are rules which need to use the enter command to get data before they run and so it is set to false by default.

Log Informs only

The PESYS system allows the user to keep a permanent record of the inference process on a disk .LOG file. This option selects whether the system should only log those results that are given an inform level of 1 and above onto disk (clauses that do not contain the inform statement are assumed to have an inform level of 0). If it is true only those conclusions marked with an inform of 1 and above are logged. If is false, all conclusions derived are logged to disk. The default is false.

Send Information to disk

This option allows one to decide whether or not to make a log on disk. If it is set to true then information (either some or all according to the previous flag) is logged onto disk, if it is false then the information is ignored. The default is true.

Return the results of expressions

This is a little used option and it simply means that if an expression is being evaluated then its result is printed on the screen. It can be used to check the accuracy or validity of results. It is set to false by default.

Start facts

This flag specifies whether the user is to be shown a list of possible values at the start of the forward chaining. If it is set to true, the system lists all the facts and the user can select which are true and which are false. The default is false.

Set the accuracy level

Since the way computers store numbers is not entirely perfect, it is often possible for two numbers to be almost exactly the same but the system would regard them as being different. The accuracy level sets the limit on how different the two numbers can be before they are considered to be different. Suppose that two numbers are stored as 1.23456 and 1.23457 and suppose that the difference in the fifth decimal place is due, simply to rounding errors on the machines part it would then be desirable for the two numbers to match - this would be done by setting the accuracy level to 4 decimal places. The accuracy works by seeing whether the difference between the two numbers is greater than or equal to the set number. So if one wanted to see whether two numbers agreed to the nearest hundred then one would set the accuracy to 100. The default value is 1e-6.

Set decimal places

When a number is written (either to the screen or to a file) the number of decimal places can be defined using this variable. The default is 2 decimal places.

File Operations

This option is only available within PESYS and it allows the user to save or load the runtime knowledge that has been derived at that time for use at another time or for examination.

7.2 How to write rules in PESYS

Since PESYS uses rules to store its knowledge, the rule structure must be as powerful, yet efficient as possible. The overall structure of the rules is shown below:

Rule Name
IF
 if clauses
THEN
 then clauses
ELSE } *OPTIONAL*
 else clauses } " "

This is the overall shape of a rule.

Rule name

The first line of a rule consists of a descriptive name. Whilst the line can be left blank, giving the rule a name can prove a considerable aid to the explanation of means of providing an answer in the same way that procedures, functions and modules are named to explain their role in the program in high level languages such as Pascal.

IF clauses

If clauses are the items that specify the knowledge in the system. In order to make this knowledge as easy to use as possible, it is advisable to make the clauses as understandable as possible. An if clause that simply says *Expert Systems* does not mean very much to the user, whilst an if clause that says *You have an interest in the field of Expert Systems* will convey far more. It is also possible to have commands as if clauses.

If clauses can be connected in a number of ways, but, unless the system is told otherwise it is assumed that the clauses are connected with the logical AND connective.

For example

Weather rule one	*Weather rule one*
if	*if*
it is raining	*it is raining*
it is cold out	*AND it is cold out*
THEN	*THEN*
it is best to stay in	*it is best to stay in*

are considered to be identical in structure, even though the first rule does not contain the word AND.

ALL the clauses connected by an AND *MUST* be true together for the rule to fire.

Alternatively a set of clauses can be connected with the OR connective. This is done by having no OR with the first clause, but adding the word OR to all the rest.

Rule all weathers	
if	
it is raining	*No OR in line*
OR it is snowing	*OR MUST be stated*
OR it is windy	*OR MUST be stated*
THEN	
it is likely to be cold	

This form of OR relationship may appear clumsy at first, but it is more powerful in the long run. The usual alternative provided is something like :

IF
the light is red or amber
THEN
you must not drive

BUT this can be rewritten as

IF
the light is red
or the light is amber
THEN
you must not drive

and the other form would not allow clauses like :

IF
it is raining
OR someone has thrown a bucket of water over your head
THEN
you will get wet

It is only necessary for one of the OR clauses to be true for that group to be true. (It does not automatically mean that the rule will be fired since it is possible to mix OR clauses and AND clauses in the same if parts). For example

IF
it is raining
OR someone has thrown a bucket of water over your head
AND you are not wearing a raincoat
THEN
you will get wet

In this example it is necessary for you to not be wearing a raincoat as well as either it raining or someone emptying a bucket of water over your head. As soon as one of the OR clauses is found to be true, all the others are ignored.

The final structure is the ATLEAST structure. This is best demonstrated with an example.

IF
atleast 2 of
you have a guaranteed money making idea
or you marry someone rich
or you rob a bank
THEN
you will get rich quickly

The ATLEAST structure is quite similar to the OR construct except that it tests all the clauses and then sees whether or not at least the required number have been found. The OR construct is an ATLEAST 1 construct that stops as soon as one has been found.

As a summary :

IF	*is equivalent to*	*IF*
A		*A*
B		*AND B*
C		*AND C*
THEN		*THEN*
D		*D*

Ask A. If it is true, ask B. If B is true, ask C. If C is also true then so is D.

IF
A
OR B
OR C
THEN
D

Ask A. If it is true, then D is true. Otherwise ask B. If this is true then D. Otherwise ask C. If this is true then D.

IF
Atleast 2 of
A
OR B
OR C
THEN
D

Ask A,B,C. If the number of true ones is greater than or equal to 2 then D.

The user can also be given a prompt. Prompts are defined by adding the word Prompt to the clause and giving the prompt name (or a command) on the next line.

e.g.
IF
the machine is working prompt
check_machine

7.3 Inform Levels and Goals

How does the system know when to stop ?

All Rule Based Expert Systems are designed to try and solve problems by manipulating rules - but how do they know when a problem has been solved (as opposed to just a rule having been fired) ? One of the most common approaches is for the user to specify a number of queries or goals that the system must try and prove. The system then uses the inference engine to manipulate the rules until a rule is fired that proves (at least) one of the goals (Forward chaining) or it takes each of the goals and tries to prove them using the rules (Backward chaining). Whilst this works in practice, it has a fundamental theoretical problem in that the goals/queries are written separately from the actual rules and hence are dependent on the rules - this means that a problem of data redundancy can easily occur.

This can either occur if there are some goals for which the rules have not yet been written (or alternatively during the testing stage, those rules have been removed) or the problem can occur if new rules are added which are meant to be the end of the inferencing stage, but the goal to tell the inference engine to stop has not been added to the list of goals.

The PESYS system overcomes these problems directly by using INFORM levels. These work as follows. All the then parts of rules (and else parts, if they exist) are potentially useful information - *if it is cold outside then you had better wear a coat* - but obviously the user does not wish to inundated with all the facts that have been proven (and disproven). Thus when one is writing the rules, any clauses whose then parts the user should be informed of are marked with an Inform statement.

Each inform statement is associated with a level. At present PESYS only differentiates between level 1 and all other levels. Level 1 will be described below. For inform levels of 2 and above the user is told the information on screen (and this is also logged to disk if necessary). Examples could include :

inform 2 The problem is with the fuel supply
or
inform 2 The patient has a very high blood pressure
etc.

Inform level 1 clauses are considered to be goals and therefore if they are found to be true the system will stop the inference engine. Since the inform statements are part of the actual then clauses, problems of redundancy between the rules and goals can never occur. Examples are :

inform 1 You will become rich quickly
or
inform 1 Strategic information systems will be useful to you

7.4 Summary

In this chapter we have introduced the idea of configuring the inference engine to a particular knowledge base. We then described the structure that the rules follow, highlighting a number of powerful features that the PESYS format has.

Finally we introduce the idea of inform levels for goals of the system. With this knowledge we are ready to write some small knowledge bases (see chapter 8).

Chapter 8

Two Knowledge Bases in PESYS

8.1 Knowledge bases written using PESYS

In this chapter we introduce two knowledge bases that have been written using PESYS. In the first knowledge base we will introduce a sample domain and begin the process of writing the rules. This will be done in a top down approach to demonstrate how the structure of a rule based system lends itself to modular design.

The second knowledge base was written as part of a research paper by Kapila & Nagpal (1988) and it demonstrates how the "English" form of PESYS rules allows the user to convert regulations from a printed rule book into the PESYS format.

8.2 Writing a knowledge base in PESYS

8.2.1 The purpose of the case study

The aim of the case study is to demonstrate the power and usefulness of the PESYS expert system shell by creating a small but non trivial knowledge base and seeing how easily this is implemented on the system.

The sample knowledge base that will be used is one which aims to see whether a firm or industry has a possibility for utilising strategic information systems to gain a competitive edge over its competitors.

8.2.2 The case study

The sample knowledge base is based on an article by *Blake Ives and Gerard P. Learmonth* entitled "*The information system as a competitive weapon*". (Ives & Learmonth, 1984)

They define an application of information systems technology *strategic* if "*it changes a firm's product or the way a firm competes in an industry*".

Michael Porter identifies five major competitive forces that affect a firm :

- The threat of new entrants
- The intensity of rivalry among existing competitors
- Pressure from substitute products
- The bargaining power of buyers
- The bargaining power of suppliers

Thus to remain competitive the firms can aim for three major goals - overall cost leadership, differentiation of a product or service and focusing on a specialised niche in the market.

When one considers using Information Systems Technology (I.S.T.) then Porter's five rules can be modified to ask if I.S.T. can prevent the threat of new entrants, can reduce the intensity of rivalry amongst existing competitors etc.

The model that Ives and Learmonth have developed is based on the Customer Resource Life Cycle. This is the life cycle that involves the customer selecting, ordering, paying for and using a resource.

If one concentrates on the needs of the customer then one can use I.S.T. to enhance customer service. This leads to greater customer loyalty and hence differentiates the firm from others in the market.

The model can be split into four or thirteen stages which are shown in figure 8.1

SIMPLE MODEL	EXTENDED MODEL	DESCRIPTION
REQUIREMENTS	Establish Requirements	To determine how much o f a resource is required
	Specify	To determine the attributes of the resource
ACQUISITION	Select Source	To determine where customers will buy the resource
	Order	To order a quantity of the resource
	Authorize and pay for	To transfer funds or extend credit
	Acquire	To take possession of a resource
	Test and Accept	To ensure that a resource meets specification
STEWARDSHIP	Integrate	To add to an existing inventory
	Monitor	To control access and use of a resource
	Upgrade	To upgrade a resource if conditions change
	Maintain	To repair a resource if necessary
RETIREMENT	Transfer or Dispose	To move, return or dispose of inventory as necessary
	Account for	To monitor spending

Figure 8.1 The Customer Resource Life Cycle Model

The knowledge base was created by combining the model and the examples of I.S.T. used in each of the thirteen stages of the model to give a number of rules. The list is by no means exhaustive but it provides a basic idea of whether or not I.S.T. can be used in the firm.

If I.S.T. can be used in any of the stages then the system will inform the user with a suitable prompt - one for each of the thirteen stages.

8.2.3 Writing the actual knowledge base

By examining the extended model (figure 8.1) we can see that there are thirteen possible areas where information systems can prove to have strategic worth. If at least one of these areas can be used then we can utilise a strategic information system. This immediately suggests to us the if part of a rule:

Bring together
if
atleast 1 of
information system can establish the requirements for resources
or the resources required can be specified
or an information system can help select suppliers for resources
....
then
inform 2 the value adding potential is high in this firm
else
inform 2 the value adding potential is low in this firm

Since the determination of the value adding potential is an important factor in the analysis it would be useful to inform the user of this - hence we use inform 2 statements for the then clauses. If we wanted the analysis to stop here then we could have used inform 1 statements, but the model suggests other factors as well.

If the company has good information system resources - for example it may have an enthusiastic and able computer department - then this will affect the performance of the company. For example a firm with good information system resources and a high value adding potential should be relatively safe at that time, but it would benefit from attacking the market using its resources and the suggestions for value adding systems. Similarly a firm with low value adding potential and low resources would probably be fairly safe since there is no possibility of other firms attacking them using information systems since there are no possible areas for their use.

How can we determine the quality of information system resources. One possibility is to have a set of rules to determine this factor. A simpler way, which we will now describe, is simply to ask the user directly.

PESYS allows for the input of variables, both numeric and string. Clearly in this case we would want a string variable (although it would be possible to use a number). In order to obtain the value of the variable (quality_of_i_s_resources$) the statement *enter quality_of_i_s_resources$* must be added to the rules. If we add it after the determination of the value adding potential, the system will determine what that potential is and then ask the user for the quality of resources. Note that the modularity of the system means that the information about where the response is to be taken from (keyboard or file) is kept independently from the actual request for the information.

Analyse results 1
if
the value adding potential is high in this firm
enter quality_of_i_s_resources$
quality_of_i_s_resources$ = low
then
inform 1 the market is dangerous
inform 1 other firms may attack

Analyse results 2
if
the value adding potential is high in this firm
quality_of_i_s_resources$ = high
then
inform 1 the market is safe
inform 1 this firm should attack

...

Note that in the second rule it is not necessary to ask the user for the value of the variable since its value was determined by the previous rule.

The next thing to do is to determine how each of the thirteen possible ways for using information systems can be undertaken. For simplicity we will consider only the first one an information system can establish the requirements for resources. In the article two examples are given, the first is based on the idea of a resource analyser - a central computer program that assists the user in the selection of resources. For example a large decorating firm may have a central computer that can model how a room would look using different colour schemes, lighting etc. The second is based on an under served market and uses an information system to, for example, guide taxi drivers to those areas where it is known that there are few other drivers. Thus for an information system to establish the requirements for resources we need at least one of these to be true.

We therefore have a rule

establish requirements
if
atleast 1 of
it is possible to create a resource analyser
or an information system can direct suppliers to empty areas
then
inform 2 information system can establish the requirements for resources

Note the use of an inform level of two to tell the user that one of the thirteen possible areas has been selected but still having the inference engine continue working.

In order to specify the possible use of a resource analyser a separate rule is needed. (Notice how easily a structured approach to rule writing is appearing). One possible rule could be:

A centralised advice body
if
there is a large customer base prompt
many_cust
and the customers are homogeneous prompt
similar_cust
then
inform 2 it is possible to create a resource analyser

The word prompt in the if clauses means that there will be a prompt associated with the clause. If the user requires more information when he is asked if the customers are homogeneous he can select prompt and a textual prompt (associated with the name similar_cust) will be displayed. Again inform 2 is used to tell the user of a possible area for using information systems.

The second rule deals with the centralised allocation of resources.

Under served market
if
the suppliers of a service are distributed randomly prompt
random_dist
then
inform 2 an information system can direct suppliers to empty areas

In this case the prompt associated with random_dist will give the examples of taxis etc.

One final rule that we could add, based on an example given in the paper, is that if a resource analyser is created then it would be possible for this analyser to also prepare sales proposals. This information could be added to the centralised advice body rule, but it is more useful (increased modularity, less redundancy) if it is written as a separate rule. In order that this rule is fired, we need to specify that the system uses mixed chaining. That is it proceeds backwards to try and prove the inform 1 statements, but that it also uses forward chaining to see if any other *useful* information can be derived.

Advice also allows the creation of orders
if
it is possible to create a resource analyser
then
inform 2 the system may also allow the preparation of sales proposals

In this particular example, this extra facility is shown using an inform level of 2. In some cases, however, we may wish to use this facility of firing rules by forward chaining to stop the inference engine. If the then clause was given an inform level of 1 and its if parts were true then the inference would then stop. For example

can't cope with stock market crash
if
the percentage drop in value is more than 15%
then
inform 1 The system is not meant to cope with this sort of data

8.2.4 The full knowledge base

A centralised advice body
if
there is a large customer base prompt
Many_cust
and the customers are homogeneous prompt
similar_cust
then
inform 2 it is possible to create a resource analyser

advice also allows the creation of orders
if
it is possible to create a resource analyser
then
inform 2 the system may also allow the preparation of sales proposals

under served market
if
the suppliers of a service are distributed randomly prompt
random_dist
then
inform 2 an information system can direct suppliers to empty areas

establish requirements
if
atleast 1 of
it is possible to create a resource analyser
or an information system can direct suppliers to empty areas
then
inform 2 information system can establish the requirements for resources

do inventories
if
there are many items available prompt
many_items
then
inform 2 there is a possibility of creating an inventory handler

do request for quotation
if
there is a possibility of creating an inventory handler
and there are many suppliers prompt
many_suppliers
then
inform 2 the system can dispatch request for quotation notes

do specify
if
there is a possibility of creating an inventory handler
then
inform 2 the resources required can be specified

allow for similar goods from different suppliers
if
a resource has been chosen prompt
choose_resource
and there are many suppliers prompt
many_suppliers
then
inform 2 an information system may suggest similar alternatives
inform 2 an information system may display the available choices

do select a source
if
an information system may display the available choices
then
inform 2 an information system can help select suppliers for resources

rule name
if
there is a large customer base prompt
many_cust
and orders are easily specified prompt
specify_easily
then
inform 2 it is possible to create a round the clock order entry system

do ordering
if
it is possible to create a round the clock order entry system
then
inform 2 an information system can assist in ordering resources

credit authorisation
if
payments for resources require credit authorisation prompt
need_auth
and there is a large customer base prompt
many_cust
then
inform 2 an information system can be used to provide automatic credit authorisation

point of sale
if
there are many suppliers prompt
many_suppliers
and there is a large customer base prompt
many_cust
and the payment system has been automated prompt
auto_pay
then
inform 2 information systems can debit customers accounts automatically

point of sale to pay for
if
atleast 1 of
information systems can debit customers accounts automatically
or an information system can be used to provide automatic credit authorisation
then
inform 2 a system could allow for the payment of bills

teller machines
if
the resources are to be dispensed on request prompt
on_req
then
inform 2 there is a possibility to utilise automatic teller machines

computer readable form
if
the resources are readable by computer prompt
comp_readable
then
inform 2 the resources can be sold as computer software

computer readable form used to acquire
if
atleast 1 of
there is a possibility to utilise automatic teller machines
or the resources can be sold as computer software
then
inform 2 an information system can be used to acquire resources

matching
if
there are many suppliers prompt
many_suppliers
and there are many items available prompt
many_items
and there are problems in finding suppliers prompt
suitable_supplier
then
inform 2 a system can be used to match resources and suppliers

check for interaction
if
a system can be used to match resources and suppliers
and the resource can react with other resources prompt
reacting_resource
then
inform 2 the system can warn the user about any problems

use match and check
if
the system can warn the user about any problems
then
inform 2 an information system can be used to test and accept resources

add to inventory
if
there is a possibility of creating an inventory handler
and there is a link between the supplier and customer prompt
link_up
then
inform 2 customers can be told that resources are in transit
inform 2 customers can add the resources to their stocks on arrival

use inventory
if
customers can add the resources to their stocks on arrival
then
inform 2 an automatic inventory controller can be created

monitor unsold resources
if
unsold resources are returned prompt
return_unsold
then
inform 2 a model can be made of sales

use model
if
a model can be made of sales
then
inform 2 an information system can be created to monitor the resources

respond to market changes
if
the market changes prompt
changing_mkt
a model can be made of sales
then
inform 2 customers can be advised about the changing markets

market changes so change shelf arrangement
if
customers can be advised about the changing markets
then
inform 2 customers can vary their stock levels
inform 2 customers can vary their sales displays

do upgrade if necessary
if
customers can be advised about the changing markets
then
inform 2 an information system can be used to upgrade the resources if necessary

annual activities
if
the resource has regular activities prompt
regular_acts
then
inform 2 the system can dispatch reminder notices

regular activities
if
the resource has periodic activities prompt
periodic_acts
then
inform 2 the system can record all of these activities

maintain through reminders
if
atleast 1 of
the system can dispatch reminder notices
or the system can record all of these activities
then
inform 2 the system can maintain the supply of resources

return a resource
if
a resource must be returned after use prompt
return_after
then
inform 2 a system can be created to be a receipt generator

return to transfer or dispose
if
a system can be created to be a receipt generator
then
inform 2 a system can be made to dispose of resources

itemised bill
if
a customer regularly buys items prompt
regular_buyer
then
inform 2 an information system can provide an itemised bill

use bill to account for
if
an information system can provide an itemised bill
then
inform 2 it is possible to create a system to account for expenditure

Bring together
if
atleast 1 of
information system can establish the requirements for resources
or the resources required can be specified
or an information system can help select suppliers for resources
or an information system can assist in ordering resources
or a system could allow for the payment of bills
or an information system can be used to acquire resources
or an information system can be used to test and accept resources
or an automatic inventory controller can be created
or an information system can be created to monitor the resources
or an information system can be used to upgrade the resources if necessary
or the system can maintain the supply of resources
or a system can be made to dispose of resources
or it is possible to create a system to account for expenditure
then
inform 2 the value adding potential is high in this firm
else
inform 2 the value adding potential is low in this firm

```
analyse results 1
if
the value adding potential is high in this firm
enter quality_of_i_s_resources$
quality_of_i_s_resources$ = low
then
inform 1 the market is dangerous
inform 1 other firms may attack

analyse results 2
if
the value adding potential is high in this firm
quality_of_i_s_resources$ = high
then
inform 1 the market is safe
inform 1 this firm should attack

analyse results 3
if
the value adding potential is low in this firm
quality_of_i_s_resources$ = high
then
inform 1 this firm should explore the possibilities

analyse results 4
if
the value adding potential is low in this firm
quality_of_i_s_resources$ = low
then
inform 1 the firm is safe
```

8.2.5 The prompts associated with the knowledge base

These prompts are associated with the knowledge base and can be displayed when certain questions are asked.
Many_cust Ie there is a large demand for the good from many sources
Similar_cust Ie if the good is not very varied or there is a regular demand
Random_dist An example is taxi drivers who cruise random areas
Many_items A process involves lots of different parts

Many_suppliers There are a number of firms who can provide the required parts
Choose_resource The type of required resource has been decided
Specify_easily For example if the resources have special names or code-numbers
Need_auth Are credit cards (either national or store-based) being used
Auto_pay Is firm-based credit card system in operation
On_req Examples include money, airline and ski-lift tickets and store coupons
Comp_readable Examples include magazines on disk and dial-up networks
Suitable_supplier Suppliers have different discount rates for example
Reacting_resource Certain prescribed medicines may react with other drugs
Link_up There is a computer or manual link between supplier and customer
Return_unsold Examples here include magazines and newspapers
Changing_mkt The number of sales changes considerably for some unknown reason
Regular_acts For example annual maintenance contract renewals
Periodic_acts For example regular services of automobiles
Return_after Examples include hire-car return and hotel key return
Regular_buyer An example is a regular drug purchase

8.3 Writing a knowledge base from an existing rulebook

The knowledge base described in this section is a cricketing rule base. In particular it focuses on those instances where a batsman is, or is not out in a game of cricket. The domain itself is well structured (the formal rules can be obtained form Wisden - the Cricketers' Almanac) (Wisden, 1983) and is fairly stable over time.

The knowledge base is called "How's That?". The name is derived from one of the cricketing rules in the area of appeals. The umpires are not allowed to give a batsman out unless an appeal has been made by the fielding side. An appeal of "How's That?" covers all the ways of being out.

8.3.1 How a batsman can be out

In cricket there are fourteen different ways in which a batsman can be out. These include being bowled, handling the ball, hitting the ball twice, being run out etc. At first sight, it would therefore appear that the system simply had to check each of the different ways until one of these was found to be true. It is, however, possible for a batsman to be out in more than one way so the system uses an atleast 1 structure in a similar way to the previous knowledge base.

How's that
if
atleast 1 of
the batsman/striker is out bowled
or the batsman is out timed out by the umpire at the bowler's end
or the batsmen is out caught
...
then
inform 1 the batsman is out

Using a top down approach, the first rule needed is to determine how a batsman can be out bowled. By examining the rule in its PESYS form, it can be seen how similar it is to the rule book version :

Law 29
The cricketer shall be out bowled if

a - his wicket is down even if the ball first touches his bat or person
b - he breaks his wicket by hitting or kicking the ball on to it before completion of a stroke, or as a result of attempting to guard his wicket.

which has an associated PESYS rule form of :

out bowled
if
atleast 1 of
the wicket is bowled down even if the ball first touches the bat
or the wicket is bowled down even if the ball first touches the batsman
or the batsman breaks his wicket by hitting the ball onto it before completion of a stroke
or the batsman breaks his wicket by kicking the ball onto it before completion of a stroke
or the batsman breaks his wicket as a result of attempting to guard his wicket
then
inform 2 the batsman/striker is out bowled

As can be seen by examining the PESYS rule given, this is an almost complete mapping from the official rule into its PESYS format. The only steps that must be taken are the separation of nested conditions - for example *his wicket is down even if the ball first touches his bat or person* is separated out into *the wicket is bowled down even if the ball first touches the bat* and *or the wicket is bowled down even if the ball first touches the batsman* and the use of an inform level 2 statement to notify the user that the batsman is out a particular way.

The full knowledge base lists all the cases for all the different ways that a batsman can be out and it is given in appendix I.

8.4 Summary

This chapter has introduced two case studies using the PESYS rule format. As well as providing an introduction into a structured methodology for rule writing, it has also demonstrated the ease of writing and understandability of the rules.

Chapter 9

An Introduction to LISP

9.1 A brief introduction to LISP

The aim of this chapter is to provide a brief introduction to the LISP programming language. For more details refer to Doukidis et al. (1988) and Winston & Horn (1984). It is hoped that this introduction will be sufficient to allow you to "follow" the Lisp listings for the Expert System program described in Chapter 10. The Lisp used in these two chapters is based on muLISP (which is a trademark of Soft Warehouse Inc.). muLISP is a general purpose Lisp system for personal computers that incorporates ideas from Common Lisp. With the incorporation of Common Lisp, muLISP provides a standardised approach to Lisp and therefore the Lisp described here should be portable between most versions of Lisp currently available. Whilst most conventional programming languages are predominantly concerned with the manipulation of numbers, Lisp is designed to allow symbol manipulation.

9.1.1 The data structures used in Lisp

Lisp has only one data structure - the symbolic expression - (s-expression). These s-expressions can be either atoms or lists. Atoms are the most basic form of s-expression since they cannot be broken down into smaller units. Atoms can either be numbers or symbols. For example

5 is a numeric atom
Green is a symbolic atom

The other form that an s-expression can take is that of a list. A list consists of a left parenthesis, followed by zero or more atoms or lists (ie more s-expressions), followed by a right parenthesis. Obviously lists can be broken up into smaller components. For example

(THIS IS A SYMBOLIC EXPRESSION) is a list made up of five atoms, whilst *(YOU CAN HAVE (LISTS WITHIN) LISTS)* is a list made up of four atoms and one list. Finally a list is empty when it has zero elements. This is usually written as *()*. In Lisp this is replaced by *NIL*. It is important to note that a list in Lisp must be perfectly balanced, that is it must have the same number of left and right parenthesis.

Special functions exist to determine whether or not an s-expression is a list or an atom. These are described in section 9.1.4.

9.1.2 The Lisp Interpreter

Lisp is primarily an interpreted language, that is a special program reads each line of Lisp code, converts it into machine code and runs it before obtaining the next line. (Compilers for Lisp also exist, for example a compiler is available for muLISP).

The Lisp interpreter reads an s-expression and prints back another s-expression that is related to it. For example if the s-expression is a function call, the interpreter prints back the s-expression that is returned by the function. The Lisp interpreter is contained in one of the primary functions in Lisp called EVAL. It evaluates the s-expressions which are given as arguments to the function. Numeric atoms, T and NIL are evaluated to themselves. If, however, the s-expression is a list, where the first element is the name of a function and the remaining elements are arguments to this function, the arguments will be evaluated first and only then will the function be called.

(EVAL 4) returns 4 since 4 is a numeric atom

(EVAL T) returns T since this is a special symbolic atom

(EVAL (PLUS 4 3)) returns 7. Firstly the arguments of the function are evaluated. These are the numbers 4 and 3 and they return themselves. Finally the function PLUS is called with these arguments.

(EVAL (PLUS 2 (PLUS 4 3))) This returns 9, firstly the function evaluates 4 and 3, calls PLUS which returns 7 and passes this value with the evaluation of 2 to the second PLUS function which returns 9.

How do you prevent EVAL from over-doing its work? When should data be treated as data and not data to be evaluated? This is done by Quoting the symbols. Quoting makes the symbols, however complex, evaluate to themselves.

In most versions of Lisp the EVAL function is embedded in the Lisp interpreter and the fact that the system is waiting for a s-expression to evaluate is shown by a $ sign.

Quoting is often used in the Lisp function to make assignments, SETQ. For example

(SETQ L '(A B)) will assign the value (A B) (since it was quoted) to the symbol L.

(SETQ L (PLUS 3 4)) will assign the value 7 to the symbol L since there was no quoting.

9.1.3 Manipulating the elements of a List

So far, we have talked about the various types of objects in Lisp. We now introduce those functions that extract elements from lists, insert elements into lists etc.

To extract elements from a list we can use the functions CAR and CDR. The function CAR extracts the first element, whilst CDR returns the sublist formed by excluding the first element. For example

```
$ (SETQ L '(A B C))
(A B C)
$ (CAR L)
A
$ (CDR L)
(B C)
$ (SETQ M '((A B) C))
((A B) C)
$ (CAR M)
(A B)
```

```
$ (CDR M)
(C)
```

In some cases it may be necessary to combine these functions. For example the second item of a list is the CAR of the CDR of the list. This can be implemented by nesting the CAR and CDR functions :

```
$ (SETQ L '(A B C))
(A B C)
$ (CAR (CDR L))
B
```

but it is also possible to use predefined functions made by combining the CAR and CDR terms. The function needed for the previous problem is CADR. Note that the order of appearance of the CARs and CDRs is the reverse of their application. The general form of the function is CXR where X can be either A or D up to a certain depth. In muLISP this is four - for example CAADDR.

```
$ (CADR L)
B
$ (CADDR L)
C
```

To insert elements into a list we can use the function CONS. This adds elements to the beginning of a list. In some cases it is necessary to create a list out of an arbitrary s-expression. LIST fulfils this function. The APPEND function joins two lists together. Examples of these three functions are shown below:

```
$ (SETQ L '(A B C))
(A B C)

$ (CONS 'X L)
(X A B C)
$ A
A
$ (LIST 'A)
(A)
```

```
$ (SETQ L '(A B))
(A B)
$ (SETQ M '(C D))
(C D)
$ (APPEND L M)
(A B C D)
```

9.1.4 Predicate functions

These are used for establishing certain conditions in a Lisp program. They return T (True) or NIL (False).

As was indicated earlier, functions exists to state-whether an s-expression is a list or an atom. The function ATOM returns T if its argument is an atom and NIL otherwise. Similarly LISTP returns T if its argument is a list and NIL otherwise.

```
$ (ATOM 'A)
T
$ (ATOM '(A B))
NIL

$ (LISTP 'A)
NIL
$ (LISTP '(A B))
T
```

The function NULL returns T if the argument evaluates to NIL, or is an empty list. Otherwise it returns NIL. AND returns NIL if any of its arguments evaluates to NIL. Similarly the OR function returns NIL if all of the arguments evaluate to NIL. NOT returns T if its argument is NIL, and NIL if it is not.

```
$ (NULL '())
T
$ (NULL '(A B))
NIL
```

```
$ (NULL NIL)
T

$ (AND T T)
T
$ (AND T NIL)
NIL

$ (OR T T)
T
$ (OR T NIL)
T
$ (OR NIL NIL)
NIL

$ (NOT T)
NIL
$ (NOT NIL)
T
```

If a program is to compare to s-expressions there are two forms that can be used. The first is EQUAL and the second is EQL. EQUAL is a fairly flexible comparison in that the only condition it places on two s-expressions being the "same" is that they print out the same. For example

```
$ (SETQ L '(A B C))
(A B C)
$ (EQUAL L L)
T
$ (EQUAL L '(A B C))
T
$ (EQUAL L '(X Y Z))
F
```

EQL, on the other hand, is far stricter in that the lists must not only match symbol by symbol, but that the actual memory locations must be the same. For example

```
$ (SETQ L '(A B C))
(A B C)
$ (EQL L L)     ; both arguments point to the same memory
                ; locations
T
$ (EQL L '(A B C)) ; although both arguments contain the
                   ; same symbols, the second argument is a
                   ; new copy and therefore does not match.
NIL
```

9.2 Functions in LISP

The only modules that are allowed in Lisp are functions. Any number of parameters can be passed to the functions and copies of the parameters are used within the function. That is the parameters are all value type parameters and not the variable type parameters that can exist in Pascal. However, this limitation can be overcome by using global variables. Global variables (usually assigned using SETQ) are those variables used within a function that are not listed in the arguments of the function. Since they are not listed, they are the actual values of the variables and not copies passed to the functions.

The Lisp functions that have been introduced previously demonstrate the method for calling functions. The general form is

(function-name argument-1 argument-2 ... argument-n)

For example

(NULL 'A) where NULL is the function name and 'A is the argument that has been passed to the function.

To define a new function in Lisp you use the DEFUN function. It has a general format :

```
(DEFUN Function-name Parameter-list
    Commands)
```

The function-name must always be an atom. The parameter list contains the variables that are assigned to the values specified when the function was called. Finally the commands are evaluated as a list of Lisp expressions. The value of the last expression evaluated is returned as the result of the function.

For example

```
(DEFUN IS-THE-LIST-EMPTY (THE-LIST-PASSED)
   (NULL THE-LIST-PASSED))
```

Here we can see that the function is called IS-THE-LIST-EMPTY. It has one argument THE-LIST-PASSED and the commands consist of one function NULL. The result of this function is returned as the result of IS-THE-LIST-EMPTY.

```
$ (IS-THE-LIST-EMPTY '(A B))
NIL
$ (IS-THE-LIST-EMPTY '())
T
```

9.2.1 Conditionals in Lisp

So far the commands described have been evaluated in a linear fashion. Most real world problems require the program to choose between different paths. The COND function allows you to specify which one of several commands in a Lisp statement is to be executed. The general form of COND is :

```
(COND
 (condition-1 expressions)
 (condition-2 expressions)
 ...
 (condition-n expressions))
```

Each list (condition-i expressions) is a clause and Lisp examines each clause separately. If the condition part of a clause evaluates to T (True) or non NIL, COND will evaluate the expressions that are associated with it and return the result of the last expression. If the condition returns NIL (False), COND skips the expressions and examines the next clause.

In a COND statement the clause form (T expression) is very useful. In this case the condition will always be true and when COND reaches this clause, the expressions will always be evaluated. This clause is often placed at the end of a COND statement so that it will be reached only if all the other conditional parts return false. Thus it can be considered as a catch-all otherwise statement. For example

```
(DEFUN IS-THE-LIST-TWO-ELEMENTS-LONG (THE-LIST)
(COND ((NULL THE-LIST) NIL )   ; return NIL if the list is
                               ; empty
   ((ATOM THE-LIST) NIL )   ; return NIL if there is only
                               ; one element
   ((NULL (CDR (CDR THE-LIST))) T) ; If the CDR of the CDR of
```

the list is empty then return true. That is if the second element of the list formed by taking the second element of the original list is empty, return true. For example

(A B C) is the original list.
(B C) is the CDR of the original list.
(C) is the CDR of the CDR of the original list.

```
   (T NIL))) ; Otherwise return NIL.
```

9.2.2 Recursion

Recursion is the process whereby a function calls itself in order to carry out a task. In general the function will call itself with a slightly less complex form of the problem. The function halts when a trivial case is presented as an argument and the system can therefore solve the problem without any further calls to itself.

For example the function to delete an item from a list that was given in chapter 4 is a recursive function.

```
(DEFUN DELETE (ITEM LST)
 (COND ((NULL LST) NIL)
    ((EQL (CAR LST) ITEM) (CDR LST))
    (T (CONS (CAR LST) (DELETE ITEM (CDR LST))))))
```

Consider the evaluation of this function with (A B C D) as the list and B as the value to be deleted.

DELETE B (A B C D)
(NULL LST) is false
(EQUAL (CAR LST) ITEM) is false
Save the CAR of the list.

Call delete with B and the CDR of the list - B C D. Thus we are recursively calling DELETE with a simpler (shorter) form of the original problem.

DELETE B (B C D)
(NULL LST) is false

(EQUAL (CAR LST) ITEM) is true, so return the CDR of the list which is (C D) and leave this level.

CONS the saved value - A - with the returned value (C D) and finish return the result (A C D).

Another recursive function is MEMBER. This tests whether the value of the first list argument is an element of the list denoted by the second argument : (MEMBER item lst). The algorithm used is:

If the lst is empty then return NIL.
If the item is equal to the CAR of the lst, return T.
Otherwise, find out if the item is a MEMBER of the CDR of the lst.

The function is therefore defined as :

```
(DEFUN MEMBER (ITEM LST)
 (COND
   ((NULL LST) NIL)
   ((EQUAL ITEM (CAR LST)) T)
   (T (MEMBER ITEM (CDR LST))) ))
```

Consider the execution of MEMBER 'B '(A B C D)

(NULL '(A B C D)) is false.
(EQUAL 'B 'A) is false.
call MEMBER with 'B '(B C D)

```
(NULL '(B C D)) is false
(EQUAL 'B B) is true so return T
```

return T.

9.2.3 Iteration

A second method for approaching a problem is to use Iteration. Here the same sequence of tasks is performed within the function, rather than calling a different function. The function simply loops through the steps using simpler arguments. Iterative control is supported by a function called LOOP.

```
(LOOP
 (argument-1)
 (argument-2)
 ...
 (argument-n))
```

When the last argument of the Loop has been evaluated, control returns to the first argument in the list. It is possible to leave the loop at any time by placing a conditional statement at the head of the argument list. If the condition evaluates to T or some non NIL value, the loop is exited. For example

```
(DEFUN DELETE (ITEM THE-LIST NEW-LIST)
(LOOP ((NULL THE-LIST) NEW-LIST)
   ((EQUAL (CAR THE-LIST) ITEM) (SETQ NEW-LIST (APPEND
NEW-LIST (CDR THE-LIST))) NEW-LIST)
   (SETQ NEW-LIST (APPEND NEW-LIST (LIST (CAR THE-
LIST))))
   (SETQ THE-LIST (CDR THE-LIST))))
```

is an iterative version of the function DELETE. It loops through the arguments, exiting if the list is empty in which case it returns the new list. If the item to be deleted has been found it adds the CDR of the list to the new list and leaves. Otherwise it simply adds the first element of the old list to the new list and shortens the old list.

9.3 Association Lists

In Lisp, every symbolic atom has a property list associated with it. It is a set of properties that are associated with the atom. Each property has a property name (which must be a symbol) and a property value (which can be any data type). For instance we can associate a property SEX with the value MALE.

One common way of implementing property lists in a program is to use association lists. An association list is a list of lists. Each sublist is called an ENTRY and the first element of each sublist is its KEY. For example, in the list :

a-list ((r red) (b blue) (g green))

r,g,b are the KEYS and red, green and blue are the values associated with each key respectively.

ASSOC is a function that takes two arguments. The first argument is a key and the second argument is the association list. ASSOC find the information in the association list via the given key. Note that ASSOC returns the whole entry including the key. If a key cannot be found, ASSOC returns NIL.

```
$ (SETQ L '((A APPLE) (B BANANA) (C CHERRY)))
((A APPLE) (B BANANA) (C CHERRY))

$ (ASSOC 'A L)
(A APPLE)

$ (ASSOC 'D L)
NIL              ; function cannot find an element with key D

$ (CDR (ASSOC 'B L))
(BANANA)
```

9.4 Input and Output in Lisp

9.4.1 Input functions

The primary input function in Lisp is READ. This function accepts information from the user via the terminal keyboard. This function reads in one complete s-expression and returns it. READ does not evaluate what it reads.

```
$ (READ)  ; user types (A B)
(A B)
$ (SETQ L (READ))  ; user types (A B) - note no quote is necessary
(A B)
```

muLISP also provides a number of other primitive input functions. READ-ATOM reads a token from the terminal. Similarly READ-LINE reads characters from the terminal until an end of line character is encountered. READ-CHAR reads a character from the terminal and returns a symbol corresponding to it.

9.4.2 Output functions

Unlike input functions Lisp has more than one output function. The main ones are PRINT, PRINC and TERPRI.

PRINT takes one argument, issues a carriage return, prints the argument on the screen followed by a space and then returns the argument as its function result. PRINC is similar except that it does not print any white spaces and it does not issue a carriage return. TERPRI is a simple function to issue a carriage return.

9.5 Summary

In this chapter we have introduced the basic principles of Lisp programming. It has described the basic principles of Lisp programming. The lists that are made up of s-expressions. Some basic functions to manipulate these s-expressions have been described as well as some tests of properties of the lists. The calling and writing of functions has been described as well as the concepts of conditional branching, iteration and recursion.

This introduction to Lisp is meant as a guide to the actual Lisp expert system that will be described in chapter 10.

Chapter 10

A Simple Expert System in LISP

10.1 Introduction

In this chapter we will develop a simple Expert System using the programming language LISP. Chapter 9 introduced the basic concepts of LISP and they will be used in the system. In this chapter we will describe a simple expert system that has been written in Lisp.

In order to demonstrate the various facilities and functions in the system we will use a very simple knowledge base that was first described in Winston (Winston, 1984). In this knowledge base we are in a Zoo and there are seven different animals. The Expert System must therefore help us to decide which of the animals we are looking at by determining various characteristics that we can see. The system will then use these characteristics to decide (where possible) which of the animals we are looking at. The possible animals are Cheetah, Tiger, Giraffe, Zebra, Ostrich, Penguin and Albatross.

Winston gives a set of 15 rules to determine which of the animals we are looking at. We will now list them together with some comments to explain them further.

Four of the rules are there to determine the biological class, MAMMAL or BIRD.

IDENTIFY1
IF
ANIMAL HAS HAIR
THEN
ANIMAL IS MAMMAL

IDENTIFY2
IF
ANIMAL GIVES MILK
THEN
ANIMAL IS MAMMAL

IDENTIFY3
IF
ANIMAL HAS FEATHERS
THEN
ANIMAL IS BIRD

IDENTIFY4
IF
ANIMAL CAN FLY
ANIMAL LAYS EGGS
THEN
ANIMAL IS BIRD

Note that in the last rule there are two if statements that have to be true for the ANIMAL to be a BIRD. Some mammals fly and some reptiles lay eggs. But only birds do both.

Once it has been determined that the animal is mammal, two rules determine whether or not the ANIMAL IS CARNIVORE.

IDENTIFY5
IF
ANIMAL IS MAMMAL
ANIMAL EATS MEAT
THEN
ANIMAL IS CARNIVORE

IDENTIFY6
IF
ANIMAL IS MAMMAL
ANIMAL HAS POINTED TEETH
ANIMAL HAS CLAWS
ANIMAL HAS FORWARD EYES
THEN
ANIMAL IS CARNIVORE

The remaining two mammal are ungulates, thus if the system fails to prove that the animal is carnivore it will try to prove that the ANIMAL IS UNGULATE. Two rules are used to determine this.

IDENTIFY7
IF
ANIMAL IS MAMMAL
ANIMAL HAS HOOFS
THEN
ANIMAL IS UNGULATE

IDENTIFY8
IF
ANIMAL IS MAMMAL
ANIMAL CHEWS CUD
THEN
ANIMAL IS UNGULATE
ANIMAL IS EVEN TOED

Rule 8 shows the possibility of having more than one then statement in a rule. The next two rules identify specific carnivores, cheetahs and tigers.

IDENTIFY9
IF
ANIMAL IS CARNIVORE
COLOR OF ANIMAL IS TAWNY
ANIMAL HAS DARK SPOTS
THEN
ANIMAL IS CHEETAH

IDENTIFY10
IF
ANIMAL IS CARNIVORE
COLOR OF ANIMAL IS TAWNY
ANIMAL HAS BLACK STRIPES
THEN
ANIMAL IS TIGER

Notice that both the tiger and the cheetah have the same color, tawny. This presents no problems since there are other distinguishing features.

The next two rules identify specific ungulates, giraffes and zebras.

IDENTIFY11
IF
ANIMAL IS UNGULATE
ANIMAL HAS LONG NECK
ANIMAL HAS LONG LEGS
ANIMAL HAS DARK SPOTS
THEN
ANIMAL IS GIRAFFE

IDENTIFY12
IF
ANIMAL IS UNGULATE
ANIMAL HAS BLACK STRIPES
THEN
ANIMAL IS ZEBRA

If the animal has been determined as being a bird then it can either be an ostrich, a penguin or an albatross.

```
IDENTIFY13
IF
ANIMAL IS BIRD
ANIMAL CAN NOT FLY
ANIMAL HAS LONG NECK
ANIMAL HAS LONG LEGS
COLOR OF ANIMAL IS BLACK AND WHITE
THEN
ANIMAL IS OSTRICH

IDENTIFY14
IF
ANIMAL IS BIRD
ANIMAL CAN NOT FLY
ANIMAL CAN SWIM
COLOR OF ANIMAL IS BLACK AND WHITE
THEN
ANIMAL IS PENGUIN

IDENTIFY15
IF
ANIMAL IS BIRD
ANIMAL FLIES WELL
THEN
ANIMAL IS ALBATROSS
```

Again two of the three birds can not fly and have the same colour. However, they have other distinct characteristics through which they can be identified. Figure 10.1 shows the relationship between the rules, it shows which rules are goals, and which rules provide information for other rules.

Winston's description stops here. Our LISP model, however, has a number of extra features that enable the system to become more powerful. These extra features are added to make the system appear more intelligent, they prevent the system from asking *silly* questions. The first extension is that the data is separated into three sets - those statements in the if and then parts of rules which have no specific format, those that represent is/are relationships and those that represent has/have relationships. For example, ANIMAL LAYS EGGS and ANIMAL CAN FLY have no special format, ANIMAL IS

MAMMAL has an is/are format and ANIMAL HAS HAIR has a has/have format.

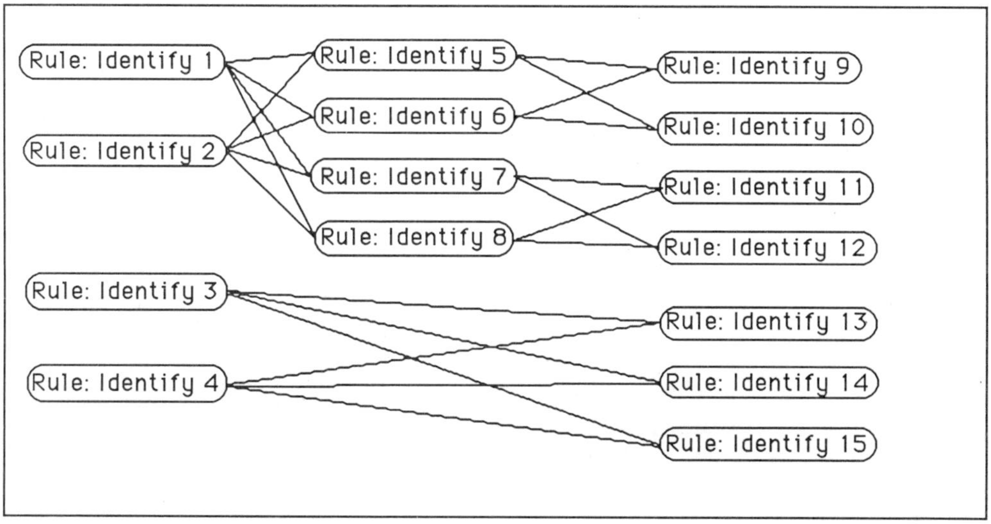

Figure 10.1 The relationship between the rules

A fourth list contains a list of conflicts - ie those values that are mutually exclusive. Thus ANIMAL IS can have only one of two values (and not both). It can either be a BIRD or a MAMMAL.

The final list contains opposite statements that allow the negations of statements to be stored easily. Therefore ANIMAL CAN FLY is the opposite of ANIMAL CAN NOT FLY. Those statements with the IS/ARE, HAS/HAVE form allow the system to ask a question only once, selecting the appropriate values, rather than asking a number of similar questions. For example, if there were three statements : THE BALL IS RED, THE BALL IS BLUE, THE BALL IS YELLOW, then a system that did not recognise the IS keyword, would have to ask three questions. By recognising the keyword, however, it would be possible to ask the user to select the appropriate value for THE BALL from RED, BLUE and YELLOW.

Similarly, if the user has proven that THE ANIMAL CAN NOT FLY, there is no point in asking questions about whether the animal can fly well for example.

10.2 How the system is organised

The knowledge base for the system is stored in two distinct areas. Figure 10.2 shows these areas.

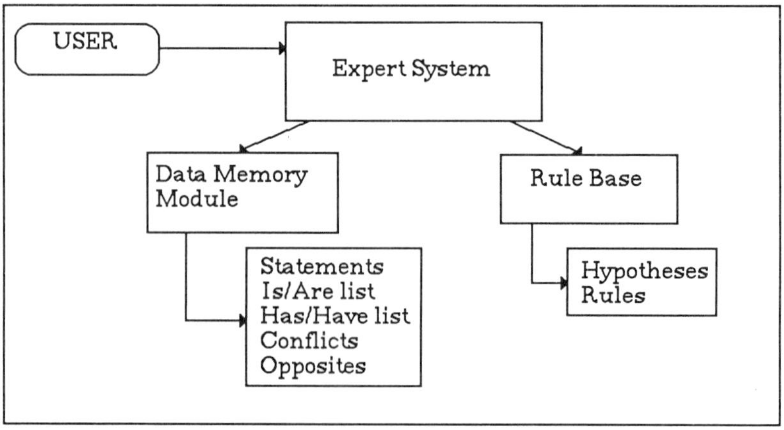

Figure 10.2 The knowledge stored in the system

10.2.1 The data memory module

The different sets of information are stored in global variables in the LISP programs. The first list contains the statements without format. We enclose these statements in lists and we make a list of these lists. By using a SETQ form we assign this data list to a global variable namely STATEMENTS.

```
(SETQ STATEMENTS '((ANIMAL GIVES MILK)
            (ANIMAL CAN FLY)
            (ANIMAL LAYS EGGS)
            (ANIMAL EATS MEAT)
            (ANIMAL CHEWS CUD)
            (ANIMAL CAN SWIM)
            (ANIMAL FLIES WELL)
            (ANIMAL DOES NOT GIVE MILK)
            (ANIMAL CAN NOT FLY)
```

```
(ANIMAL DOES NOT LAY EGGS)
(ANIMAL DOES NOT EAT MEAT)
(ANIMAL DOES NOT CHEW CUD)
(ANIMAL CAN NOT SWIM)
(ANIMAL DOES NOT FLY WELL)))
```

We do exactly the same thing for is(are) and has(have) relational statements. They are both given below. Note that the items to the left and right of the keyword such as IS, ARE, HAS and HAVE can be as long as is necessary. Therefore COLOR OF ANIMAL can be one item and BLACK AND WHITE can be another. The is/are relations are assigned to a global data list called IS-LIST. The has/have relations are assigned to a global data list called HAS-LIST using a SETQ form.

```
(SETQ IS-LIST '((ANIMAL IS ALBATROSS)
        (ANIMAL IS PENGUIN)
        (ANIMAL IS OSTRICH)
        (ANIMAL IS ZEBRA)
        (ANIMAL IS GIRAFFE)
        (ANIMAL IS TIGER)
        (ANIMAL IS CHEETAH)
        (ANIMAL IS CARNIVORE)
        (ANIMAL IS UNGULATE)
        (ANIMAL IS MAMMAL)
        (ANIMAL IS BIRD)
        (COLOR OF ANIMAL IS TAWNY)
        (COLOR OF ANIMAL IS BLACK AND WHITE)))

(SETQ HAS-LIST '((ANIMAL HAS HAIR)
        (ANIMAL HAS FEATHERS)
        (ANIMAL HAS POINTED TEETH)
        (ANIMAL HAS CLAWS)
        (ANIMAL HAS FORWARD EYES)
        (ANIMAL HAS HOOFS)
        (ANIMAL HAS DARK SPOTS)
        (ANIMAL HAS BLACK STRIPES)
        (ANIMAL HAS LONG NECK)
        (ANIMAL HAS LONG LEGS)))
```

Naturally it would be possible to use different forms of relations as well as the *is* and *has* relations used above. However, as we described in chapter 3, the *is* and *has* relations are ones primarily used in object-attribute-value triplets and semantic networks.

The conflicts list is similarly made up of lists of conflicts. Since the system again looks for the keywords it is possible to have as many words as is necessary to the left of the keyword, for example COLOR OF ANIMAL. If the conflicting values are more than one word then they must be put into a sublist, since each sublist is counted as one higher level item, for example, the last two sublists in the list below have values that are more than two words and are therefore enclosed in brackets. (BLACK AND WHITE) is one conflicting value and it is enclosed in brackets. This list of lists is assigned to global data list called CONFLICTS using the SETQ form.

```
(SETQ CONFLICTS '((ANIMAL IS UNGULATE CARNIVORE)
          (ANIMAL IS BIRD MAMMAL)
          (ANIMAL HAS HAIR FEATHERS)
          (ANIMAL HAS HOOFS CLAWS)
          (ANIMAL HAS (DARK SPOTS)(BLACK STRIPES))
          (COLOR OF ANIMAL  IS TAWNY (BLACK AND
              WHITE))))
```

Finally we have the opposite unstructured statements. These are formed by putting the first unstructured statement in a list, then the atom OPP and finally the opposite unstructured list. This is all stored in one list. Each of these opposite lists are then enclosed in a list that is assigned using SETQ to a global data list called OPPOSITES as shown below.

```
(SETQ OPPOSITES '(
((ANIMAL GIVES MILK) OPP (ANIMAL DOES NOT GIVE MILK))
((ANIMAL CAN FLY) OPP (ANIMAL CAN NOT FLY))
((ANIMAL LAYS EGGS) OPP (ANIMAL DOES NOT LAY EGGS))
((ANIMAL EATS MEAT) OPP (ANIMAL DOES NOT EAT MEAT))
((ANIMAL CHEWS CUD) OPP (ANIMAL DOES NOT CHEW CUD))
((ANIMAL CAN SWIM) OPP (ANIMAL CAN NOT SWIM))
((ANIMAL FLIES WELL) OPP (ANIMAL DOES NOT FLY WELL))))
```

10.2.2 The rule base module

Now that we have defined our background data we must define the rules that use it. The first block of facts that exist in the knowledge base are the hypotheses. There are seven hypotheses, one for each animal and they are all enclosed in lists. These lists are then enclosed in a list and are SETQ to the global data list HYPOTHESES.

```
(SETQ HYPOTHESES '((ANIMAL IS ALBATROSS)
        (ANIMAL IS PENGUIN)
        (ANIMAL IS OSTRICH)
        (ANIMAL IS ZEBRA)
        (ANIMAL IS GIRAFFE)
        (ANIMAL IS TIGER)
        (ANIMAL IS CHEETAH)))
```

Finally we must code the rules into LISP. This is done easily using the following format. Note that using the nested lists in LISP the first element (CAR) in the list is the rule name, the second element (CADR) is the list of IF statements (with the keyword IF) and the third element (CADDR) is the list of THEN statements (with the keyword THEN).

```
(IDENTIFY.....
     (IF (.. ..  ...  ....)
         (..... ......  .... )
              .
              .
         ( ...........     ))
     (THEN (... ...  ....  )
              .
              .
          ( ....... ..... ...  )))
```

We represent the rules using the above format and we enclose them in a list. A global data list called RULES is assigned to hold all the rules.

```
(SETQ RULES '(

(IDENTIFY1
   (IF (ANIMAL HAS HAIR))
   (THEN (ANIMAL IS MAMMAL)))

(IDENTIFY2
   (IF (ANIMAL GIVES MILK))
   (THEN (ANIMAL IS MAMMAL)))

(IDENTIFY3
   (IF (ANIMAL HAS FEATHERS))
   (THEN (ANIMAL IS BIRD)))

(IDENTIFY4
   (IF (ANIMAL CAN FLY)
     (ANIMAL LAYS EGGS))
   (THEN (ANIMAL IS BIRD)))

(IDENTIFY5
   (IF (ANIMAL IS MAMMAL)
     (ANIMAL EATS MEAT))
   (THEN (ANIMAL IS CARNIVORE)))

(IDENTIFY6
   (IF (ANIMAL IS MAMMAL)
     (ANIMAL HAS POINTED TEETH)
     (ANIMAL HAS CLAWS)
     (ANIMAL HAS FORWARD EYES))
   (THEN (ANIMAL IS CARNIVORE)))

(IDENTIFY7
   (IF (ANIMAL IS MAMMAL)
     (ANIMAL HAS HOOFS))
   (THEN (ANIMAL IS UNGULATE)))
```

```
(IDENTIFY8
   (IF (ANIMAL IS MAMMAL)
      (ANIMAL CHEWS CUD))
   (THEN (ANIMAL IS UNGULATE)
       (ANIMAL IS EVEN TOED)))

(IDENTIFY9
   (IF (ANIMAL IS CARNIVORE)
      (COLOR OF ANIMAL IS TAWNY)
      (ANIMAL HAS DARK SPOTS))
   (THEN (ANIMAL IS CHEETAH)))

(IDENTIFY10
   (IF (ANIMAL IS CARNIVORE)
      (COLOR OF ANIMAL IS TAWNY)
      (ANIMAL HAS BLACK STRIPES))
   (THEN (ANIMAL IS TIGER)))

(IDENTIFY11
   (IF (ANIMAL IS UNGULATE)
      (ANIMAL HAS LONG NECK)
      (ANIMAL HAS LONG LEGS)
      (ANIMAL HAS DARK SPOTS))
   (THEN (ANIMAL IS GIRAFFE)))

(IDENTIFY12
   (IF (ANIMAL IS UNGULATE)
      (ANIMAL HAS BLACK STRIPES))
   (THEN (ANIMAL IS ZEBRA)))

(IDENTIFY13
   (IF (ANIMAL IS BIRD)
      (ANIMAL CAN NOT FLY)
      (ANIMAL HAS LONG NECK)
      (ANIMAL HAS LONG LEGS)
      (COLOR OF ANIMAL IS BLACK AND WHITE))
   (THEN (ANIMAL IS OSTRICH)))
```

```
(IDENTIFY14
   (IF (ANIMAL IS BIRD)
      (ANIMAL CAN NOT FLY)
      (ANIMAL CAN SWIM)
      (COLOR OF ANIMAL IS BLACK AND WHITE))
   (THEN (ANIMAL IS PENGUIN)))

(IDENTIFY15
   (IF (ANIMAL IS BIRD)
      (ANIMAL FLIES WELL))
   (THEN (ANIMAL IS ALBATROSS)))  ))
```

10.3 A top down design approach to the expert system

Figure 10.3 shows main functions of the system. Each of these areas will be described in detail with a statement of what each function does included in the description.

10.3.1 The Top level function - Expert-Systems

The first function to examine is EXPERT-SYSTEMS. The function is the top level function of the system. It displays the opening menu to the user. The user has three options - view the data base and the knowledge base, use the forward chaining mechanism or use the backward chaining inference mechanism. Once this has been done the user has the opportunity to try any of the choices again.

If the user selects to view the data base and the knowledge base the function VALIDATION is used which controls the display of the several data base blocks and the knowledge base blocks. If the user chooses forward chaining it calls the function FORWARD-CHAINING. Similarly if the user selects backward chaining it calls BACKWARD-CHAINING. Pressing the space bar exits the system.

The full listing for the system is given in Appendix II. This chapter, however, is only meant to give an overview of the functionality of the system, not the detailed code that is used to make the system user friendly.

```
(DEFUN EXPERT-SYSTEMS (ASKED FACTS A)
 (LOOP
  (SETQ ASKED NIL) (SETQ FACTS NIL) (CLEAR-SCREEN)
   ...
   (... (CATCH NIL (VALIDATION)))
   (... (CATCH NIL (FORWARD-CHAINING)))
   (... (CATCH NIL (BACKWARD-CHAINING))))
 ...
```

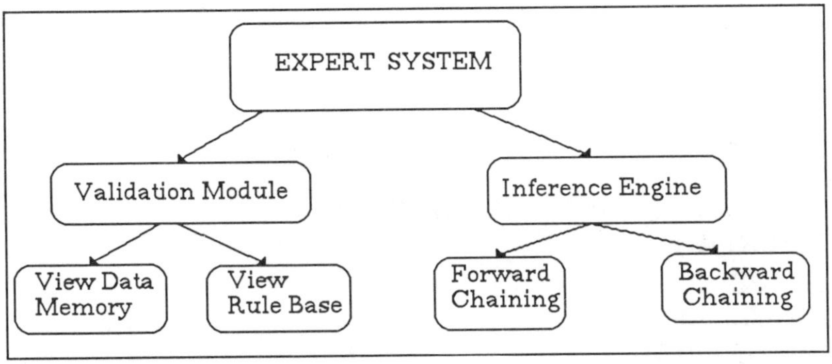

Figure 10.3 The main functions in the Expert System

10.3.2 The validation Module

The next function to examine is VALIDATION. The function is an intermediate step towards displaying the data base and the knowledge base blocks so that the user can validate them. The user is presented with two options. Either to view the data base or view the knowledge base blocks. If the user chooses to view the data base then OUTPUT calls OUTPUT-DATA-MEMORY. If the user chooses to view the knowledge base then it calls OUTPUT-KNOWLEDGE-BASE.

In OUTPUT-KNOWLEDGE-BASE the user is presented with two options he can either have the HYPOTHESES or the RULES displayed onto the screen. If the user selects to view the HYPOTHESES the function calls HELP-PRINT to display these. If the choice was to view the RULES then the function calls function OUTPUT-RULES.

The data base, as was explained previously contains five blocks of data.

Depending on the choice entered by the user the system will either display the unstructured STATEMENTS, the IS-LIST or the HAS-LIST which are printed using the HELP-PRINT function.

If the user chooses he can have the CONFLICTS displayed or the OPPOSITES displayed. These two choices use the function OUTPUT-CONS-AND-OPPS.

Given a list of lists, HELP-PRINT will PRINC NIL if the list is empty, or display all sublists without any parentheses one per line. The contents of each sublist is displayed using the function PRINTING.

```
(DEFUN HELP-PRINT (LST A)
 (COND
  ((NULL LST) (PRINC " NIL") (TERPRI))
  (T (TERPRI)
    (LOOP
     ((NULL LST))
     (SETQ A (CAR LST))
     (LOOP
      ((NULL A))
      (PRINC (CAR A))
      (PRINC " ")
      (SETQ A (CDR A)))
     (TERPRI)
     (SETQ LST (CDR LST))))))
```

PRINTING displays the contents of a list without parentheses.

```
(DEFUN PRINTING (LST)
 (LOOP
  ((NULL LST))
  (PRINC (CAR LST))
  (COND ((NOT (NULL (CDR LST))) (PRINC " ")))
  (SETQ LST (CDR LST))))
```

The following function displays the RULES free from parentheses. For example rule IDENTIFY1 will be displayed as follows:

```
IDENTIFY1
    IF ANIMAL HAS HAIR
    THEN ANIMAL IS MAMMAL
```

The function calls PRINTING to display the contents of a list free of parentheses.

```
(DEFUN OUTPUT-RULES (TEMP-RULES LST L)
 (TERPRI)
 (LOOP
  ((NULL TEMP-RULES))
  (PRINC (CAAR TEMP-RULES)) (TERPRI)
  (SETQ LST (CDAR TEMP-RULES))
  (LOOP
   ((NULL LST))
   (SETQ L (CAR LST))
   (LOOP
    ((NULL L))
    (COND
     ((ATOM (CAR L)) (PRINC (CAR L)))
     (T (PRINTING (CAR L))))
    (TERPRI)
    (SETQ L (CDR L)))
   (SETQ LST (CDR LST)))
  (TERPRI 1)
  (SETQ TEMP-RULES (CDR TEMP-RULES))))
```

OUTPUT-CONFS-AND-OPPS is the last function needed to understand the displaying of the data and knowledge base. The same function displays both the CONFLICTS and OPPOSITES. This is achieved by looking into the list either for an IS or ARE or HAS or HAVE or OPP.

```
(DEFUN OUTPUT-CONFS-AND-OPPS (LST L MARK REL)
 (TERPRI)
 (LOOP
  ((NULL LST))
  (SETQ L (CAR LST) REL NIL MARK NIL)
  (LOOP
   ((NULL L))
```

```
    (COND ((AND (NOT (EQL REL NIL)) (NOT (EQL REL MARK)))
        (PRINC ",")))
    (COND ((OR (EQL (CAR L) 'IS) (EQL (CAR L) 'ARE)
            (EQL (CAR L) 'HAS) (EQL (CAR L) 'HAVE))
        (SETQ REL (CAR L))))
    (COND ((ATOM (CAR L)) (PRINC (CAR L)) (PRINC " "))
        (T (PRINTING (CAR L)) (PRINC " ")))
    (SETQ MARK (CAR L))
    (SETQ L (CDR L)))
   (TERPRI)
   (SETQ LST (CDR LST))))
```

10.3.3 The Forward Chaining module

The basic algorithm for forward chaining was described in chapter 3.

FORWARD-CHAINING is the top level function the forward chaining inference strategy. The function gets the list of POSSIBLES by calling COLLECT-POSSIBLES. It then loops through all the rules. If the then statements include a member of the HYPOTHESIS, this will be displayed in a window.

Each then statement is then examined and if any of the conflicts of the statement (obtained by using FIND-CONFLICTS) is found in the FACTS list, the rule is abandoned and all the then parts are added to the ASKED list by calling ADD-THEN-PARTS.

If none of the then statements are in FACTS the function examines all the if statements. If any of these are found in ASKED the rule is abandoned and the then statements are added to ASKED.

If a statement is not yet known and it is in the list of POSSIBLES the function ASK-THE-USER is called to confirm its truth. If all the if statements are confirmed then the then statements are added to FACTS by using ADD-THEN-PARTS. If any of the then parts are in HYPOTHESIS then the inference process is halted and the hypothesis is displayed. If all the rules have been tried and no hypothesis has been found the system displays INSUFFICIENT INFORMATION.

The FORWARD-CHAINING and BACKWARD-CHAINING functions make use of two lists - ASKED and FACTS. The FACTS list holds, during run time, all those unstructured and relational statements that have been confirmed by the user or derived by the system. ASKED, on the other hand, holds all those statements that were rejected by the user or whose conflicts and opposites were accepted by the user.

The function COLLECT-POSSIBLES checks every rule using CHECK-IF-PART and adds all the if statements to the variable POSSIBLES using EXPAND-LIST (so that duplication is avoided).

```
(DEFUN COLLECT-POSSIBLES (RULES RLS)
 (SETQ POSSIBLES NIL RLS RULES)
 (LOOP
  ((NULL RLS))
  (SETQ POSSIBLES (EXPAND-LIST
          (CHECK-IF-PART (GET-IF-PART (CAR RLS)) RULES)
          POSSIBLES))
  (SETQ RLS (CDR RLS))))
```

EXPAND-LIST is a function whose purpose is to add new elements in a given list without duplicating. Given two lists of lists, LST1 and LST2, the function LOOPs through LST1 and adds those sublists of LST1 that are not already MEMBERs of LST2. The function returns the new LST2.

```
(DEFUN EXPAND-LIST (LST1 LST2)
  (COND
   ((NULL LST1) LST2)
   ((MEMBER (CAR LST1) LST2 'EQUAL)
    (EXPAND-LIST (CDR LST1) LST2))
   (T (EXPAND-LIST (CDR LST1) (APPEND LST2 (LIST (CAR
LST1)))))))
```

For a rule GET-IF-PART returns the if statements of that rule in a similar way to GET-THEN-PART.

```
(DEFUN GET-IF-PART (RULE)
 (CDR (ASSOC 'IF RULE)))
```

CHECK-IF-PART returns a list of all those if statements in a particular rule that are not in the then parts of other rules.

```
(DEFUN CHECK-IF-PART (IF-PARTS RULES)
 (COND
  ((NULL IF-PARTS) NIL)
  ((CHECK-THEN-PART (CAR IF-PARTS) RULES)
   (CHECK-IF-PART (CDR IF-PARTS) RULES))
  (T (CONS (CAR IF-PARTS)(CHECK-IF-PART (CDR IF-PARTS)
RULES)))))
```

CHECK-THEN-PART determines whether or not a given if statement occurs in the then parts of any rules. The function examines every rule and gets the then parts (using GET-THEN-PART) and checks to see if the IF statement is a member of the then list. If it is found in any rule the function returns true, otherwise it returns NIL.

```
(DEFUN CHECK-THEN-PART (IF-PART RULES)
  (LOOP
   ((NULL RULES) NIL)
   ((MEMBER IF-PART (GET-THEN-PART (CAR RULES)) 'EQUAL)
    T)
   (SETQ RULES (CDR RULES))))
```

GET-THEN-PART returns the then statements of a rule.

```
(DEFUN GET-THEN-PART (RULE)
 (CDR (ASSOC 'THEN RULE)))
```

The function FIND-CONFLICTS is the top level function for using the conflicting values for relational statements. The function examines the CONFLICTS list and returns the values if they exist, otherwise it returns NIL.

By calling HELP-FIND-CONFLICTS the function accesses the conflicts of the statement if they exist. If they do they are returned by a call to another function called RETURN-CONFLICTS.

```
(DEFUN FIND-CONFLICTS (A CONFL LST)
 (LOOP
  ((NULL CONFL) NIL)
  (SETQ LST (HELP-FIND-CONFLICTS A (CAR CONFL)))
  ((NOT (NULL LST)) (RETURN-CONFLICTS A LST))
  (SETQ CONFL (CDR CONFL))))
```

HELP-FIND-CONFLICTS takes as its arguments two lists which are in fact two relational statements. The first is the one that was originally supplied as an argument to FIND-CONFLICTS, the second is an entry from the CONFLICTS list. The two are compared entry by entry and if they are match to the left of a keyword - IS, ARE, HAS or HAVE the function ACCESS-CONFLICT-VALUES is used to extract the conflicts of a given statement. If the two lists do not match before the keyword the function returns NIL. If find conflicts returns NIL the system examines the next entry in CONFLICTS.

```
(DEFUN HELP-FIND-CONFLICTS (A LST)
 (COND
  ((AND (EQL (CAR A) (CAR LST))
     (OR (EQL (CAR A) 'IS) (EQL (CAR A) 'ARE)
        (EQL (CAR A) 'HAS) (EQL (CAR A) 'HAVE)))
   (ACCESS-CONFLICT-VALUES (CDR A) (CDR LST)))
  ((EQL (CAR A) (CAR LST))
   (HELP-FIND-CONFLICTS (CDR A) (CDR LST)))
  (T NIL)))
```

ACCESS-CONFLICT-VALUES returns the actual conflicting values of the relational statement's value.

```
(DEFUN ACCESS-CONFLICT-VALUES (LST1 LST2 CONFLIST)
 (LOOP
  ((NULL LST2) NIL)
  ((OR (EQUAL LST1 (CAR LST2)) (EQUAL LST1 (LIST (CAR
LST2))))
   (SETQ CONFLIST (APPEND CONFLIST (CDR LST2))))
  (SETQ CONFLIST (APPEND CONFLIST (LIST (CAR LST2)))
     LST2 (CDR LST2))))
```

RETURN-CONFLICTS makes relational statements out of the list delivered by HELP-FIND-CONFLICTS. Thus it makes (ANIMAL IS MAMMAL) (ANIMAL IS BIRD) from (ANIMAL IS MAMMAL BIRD).

```
(DEFUN RETURN-CONFLICTS (C C-LIST LST LST1)
 (LOOP
  (SETQ LST (APPEND LST (LIST (CAR C))))
  ((OR (EQL (CAR C) 'IS) (EQL (CAR C) 'ARE)
     (EQL (CAR C) 'HAS) (EQL (CAR C) 'HAVE)))
  (SETQ C (CDR C)))
 (LOOP
  ((NULL C-LIST) LST1)
  (COND
   ((ATOM (CAR C-LIST))
    (SETQ LST1 (CONS (APPEND LST (LIST (CAR C-LIST))) LST1)))
   (T (SETQ LST1 (CONS (APPEND LST (CAR C-LIST)) LST1))))
  (SETQ C-LIST (CDR C-LIST))))
```

The function FIND-OPPOSITES finds the opposite of an unstructured statement by examining the list OPPOSITES.

```
(DEFUN FIND-OPPOSITES (A LST)
 (COND
  ((NULL LST) NIL)
  ((EQUAL A (CAAR LST)) (CADDAR LST))
  ((EQUAL A (CADDAR LST)) (CAAR LST))
  (T (FIND-OPPOSITES A (CDR LST)))))
```

For a given if statement that does not occur in the then part of any rules ASK-THE-USER determines whether the statement is an unstructured statement or a relational statement and calls ASK-STATEMENT or ASK-RELATION accordingly.

```
(DEFUN ASK-THE-USER (IF-PART RULE)
 (COND
   ((MEMBER IF-PART STATEMENTS 'EQUAL)
    (ASK-STATEMENT IF-PART RULE))
   (T (ASK-RELATION IF-PART RULE))))
```

The function ADD-THEN-PARTS will add the then parts of a rule to either ASKED or FACTS and the conflicts to the other list. If the list to be used is FACTS the function calls EXPAND-LIST to add the then statements into FACTS, and it calls FIND-CONFLICTS to find the conflicting values of the relational statement and uses EXPAND-LIST to add them to ASKED. If the list to be used is ASKED it will call EXPAND-LIST to add the then statements into ASKED.

```
(DEFUN ADD-THEN-PARTS (LISTHEAD RULE TEMP CONF)
 (SETQ TEMP (GET-THEN-PART RULE))
 (COND
   ((STRING= LISTHEAD 'FACTS)
    (SETQ FACTS (EXPAND-LIST TEMP FACTS))
    (LOOP
     ((NULL TEMP) NIL)
     (SETQ CONF (FIND-CONFLICTS (CAR TEMP) CONFLICTS))
     (SETQ ASKED (EXPAND-LIST CONF ASKED))
     (SETQ TEMP (CDR TEMP))))
   ((STRING= LISTHEAD 'ASKED)
    (SETQ ASKED (EXPAND-LIST TEMP ASKED)))))
```

The function ASK-STATEMENT asks the user to confirm whether or not an unstructured statement is true. If the user types Y he is confirming the statement, N means rejection and ? asks for an explanation. If the user types Y the function adds the if statement just confirmed in the FACTS list, it calls FIND-OPPOSITES to find the opposite of the statement and puts this into the ASKED list. If the user types N then the reverse is applied. The FACTS window will be updated by calling HELP-PRINT to print the new FACTS list. If the user accepted the statement the function returns T otherwise it returns NIL.

CHECK-RELATION determines whether two relational statements are equal.

```
(DEFUN CHECK-RELATION (LST1 LST2)
 (COND
   ((AND (EQL (CAR LST1) (CAR LST2))
       (OR (EQL (CAR LST1) 'IS) (EQL (CAR LST1) 'ARE)
          (EQL (CAR LST1) 'HAS) (EQL (CAR LST1) 'HAVE))))
   ((EQL (CAR LST1) (CAR LST2))
    (CHECK-RELATION (CDR LST1) (CDR LST2)))
   (T NIL)))
```

PRINT-RELATION displays a relational statement upto and including the keyword.

```
(DEFUN PRINT-RELATION (LST PART)
 (LOOP
  (SETQ PART (APPEND PART (LIST (CAR LST))))
  ((OR (EQL (CAR LST) 'IS) (EQL (CAR LST) 'ARE)
     (EQL (CAR LST) 'HAS) (EQL (CAR LST) 'HAVE))
   (PRINTING PART))
  (SETQ LST (CDR LST)))
 (PRINC ":-"))
```

PRINT-VALUES displays the list of possible values that the relation can take.

```
(DEFUN PRINT-VALUES (LST REST)
 (LOOP
  (SETQ REST (CONS (CAR LST) REST))
  ((OR (EQL (CAR LST) 'IS) (EQL (CAR LST) 'ARE)
     (EQL (CAR LST) 'HAS) (EQL (CAR LST) 'HAVE))
   (PRINTING (CDR LST)))
  (SETQ LST (CDR LST))))
```

The function READING reads in a number or a space.

The ASK-RELATION function asks the user to confirm relational statements. It examines all the if statements in the current rule using CHECK-RELATION to see if they have the same keyword etc. as the statement being checked. All those that do are stored in a list. By typing in a number the user can choose a particular value for the relation. If the user enters ? an explanation is provided. Pressing space means that the user rejects the values shown and they are added to ASKED using EXPAND-LIST. Selecting a numbered item adds the corresponding statement to FACTS and its CONFLICTS are added to ASKED.

The function CURRENT-EXPLANATION provides information about the current stage of inference and is invoked when the user types "?" at any choice in the forward or backward chaining.

When the explanation is required the system prints out the rule name and the statement that it is currently trying to establish. All the known if statements are then displayed and then those if statements that need to be determined are displayed.

CONCLUDE displays the FACTS that have been derived during an interaction if requested.

10.3.5 The backward chaining module

The function BACKWARD-CHAINING is the top level function for this inference strategy. The function LOOPs through the HYPOTHESES and tries to prove each one. It displays the HYPOTHESES under examination in a window and then calls VERIFY to try and prove it. If a hypothesis has been proven the inferencing stops and the conclusion is displayed otherwise the next hypothesis is examined until no more hypotheses exist in which case the INSUFFICIENT INFORMATION prompt is displayed.

The COLLECT-RULES function is used in backward chaining and it finds all the rules that contain a particular statement in their then parts.

```
(DEFUN COLLECT-RULES (THEN-PART RULE-LIST)
 (COND
  ((NULL RULE-LIST) NIL)
  ((MEMBER THEN-PART (GET-THEN-PART (CAR RULE-LIST))
'EQUAL)
   (CONS (CAR RULE-LIST)
      (COLLECT-RULES THEN-PART (CDR RULE-LIST))))
  (T (COLLECT-RULES THEN-PART (CDR RULE-LIST)))))
```

The main parameter in VERIFY is the statement that is to be proven. If it is already in FACTS the function returns T otherwise COLLECT-RULES is called to extract the rules that contain the statement in their then parts (ie rules which if fired will add the statement to facts). If there are no rules and the fact is not in ASKED the user is asked about the statement using ASK-THE-USER.

If the statement does exist in some rules the system examines each rule in turn to see if it can be fired by using TRYRULE1. If the rule can be fired VERIFY returns T. If the statement cannot be proven this way, the system examines all the rules again, this time using TRYRULE2. This is similar to TRYRULE1 except that it itself uses VERIFY.

```
    (DEFUN VERIFY (FACT RULE FACT-RULES IF-PARTS SPOK
TEMP-RULES)
      ((MEMBER FACT FACTS 'EQUAL) (RETURN T))
      (SETQ FACT-RULES (COLLECT-RULES FACT RULES))
      (SETQ EXIT 'EXIT)
      (COND ((AND (NULL FACT-RULES) (NOT (MEMBER FACT
ASKED 'EQUAL)))
          (SETQ EXIT (ASK-THE-USER FACT RULE))))
      ((EQL EXIT NIL) (RETURN NIL))
      ((EQL EXIT T) (RETURN T))
      ((AND (NULL FACT-RULES) (MEMBER FACT ASKED 'EQUAL))
       (RETURN NIL))
      (SETQ SPOK NIL)
      (SETQ TEMP-RULES FACT-RULES)
      (LOOP
       ((NULL TEMP-RULES))
       (SETQ SPOK (TRYRULE1 (CAR TEMP-RULES)))
       ((EQL SPOK T))
       (SETQ TEMP-RULES (CDR TEMP-RULES)))
      ((EQL SPOK T) (RETURN T))
      (LOOP
       ((NULL FACT-RULES))
       (SETQ SPOK (TRYRULE2 (CAR FACT-RULES) FACT-RULES))
       ((EQL SPOK T))
       (SETQ FACT-RULES (CDR FACT-RULES)))
      (COND ((EQL SPOK T) (RETURN T))
```

```
((EQL SPOK NIL) (RETURN NIL))))
```

TRYRULE1 works by examining all the if parts of the rule and seeing if they are all in FACTS. If they all are it adds the then facts using ADD-THEN-PARTS and the function returns T.

```
(DEFUN TRYRULE1 (RULE IF-PARTS ONE)
  (SETQ IF-PARTS (GET-IF-PART RULE))
  (SETQ ONE T)
  (LOOP
   ((NULL IF-PARTS))
   ((NOT (MEMBER (CAR IF-PARTS) FACTS 'EQUAL)) (SETQ
ONE NIL))
   (SETQ IF-PARTS (CDR IF-PARTS)))
  (COND
   ((EQL ONE T) (ADD-THEN-PARTS 'FACTS RULE)
    (MAKE-WINDOW 1 52 23 27) (CLEAR-SCREEN)
    (PRINC "      FACTS") (TERPRI)
    (PRINC "      -----") (HELP-PRINT FACTS)
    (SETQ UP-TO-NOW (EXPAND-LIST (GET-THEN-PART RULE)
                    UP-TO-NOW))))
  (COND ((EQL ONE NIL) NIL)
     ((EQL ONE T) T)))
```

The function TRYRULE2 is very similar to TRYRULE1 except that rather than simply checking to see if a fact is known (is in FACTS) it uses VERIFY to determine the facts.

```
(DEFUN TRYRULE2 (RULE FACT-RULES TWO TCON THEN-
PARTS IF-PART)
  (SETQ THEN-PARTS (GET-THEN-PART RULE))
  (SETQ TWO T)
  (LOOP
   ((NULL THEN-PARTS))
   (SETQ TCON (FIND-CONFLICTS (CAR THEN-PARTS)
CONFLICTS))
   (LOOP
    ((NULL TCON))
    ((MEMBER (CAR TCON) FACTS 'EQUAL) (RETURN NIL))
```

```
      (SETQ TCON (CDR TCON)))
     (SETQ THEN-PARTS (CDR THEN-PARTS)))
    (SETQ IF-PARTS (GET-IF-PART RULE))
    (LOOP
     ((NULL IF-PARTS))
     (SETQ TWO (VERIFY (CAR IF-PARTS) RULE FACT-RULES IF-
PARTS))
     ((EQL TWO NIL) (RETURN NIL))
     (SETQ IF-PARTS (CDR IF-PARTS)))
    (COND
     ((EQL TWO T) (ADD-THEN-PARTS 'FACTS RULE)
      (MAKE-WINDOW 1 52 23 27) (CLEAR-SCREEN)
      (PRINC "      FACTS") (TERPRI) (PRINC "        -----")
      (HELP-PRINT FACTS)
      (SETQ UP-TO-NOW (EXPAND-LIST (GET-THEN-PART RULE)
UP-TO-NOW))
   (RETURN T))))
```

10.4 Summary

This chapter has introduced a simple expert system written in Lisp. By following the text and examining the listing in Appendix II the actual method that the system uses to manipulate the rules an good understanding of the expert system should be obtained. Since the system is written in Lisp it should be very easy to improve the system by adding extra functions, different data structures and better explanation facilities.

Appendix I - The "How's That!" Knowledge Base

The following are the rules from the "How's That!" knowledge base written using PESYS. Some rules have optional prompts but these are not detailed below.

how's that
if
atleast 1 of
the batsman/striker is out bowled
or the batsman is out timed out by the umpire at the bowler's end
or the batsman/striker is out caught
or the batsman is out handled the ball
or the batsman is out hit the ball twice
or the batsman is out returning the ball to a fieldsman
or the batsman is out hit wicket
or the batsman is out lbw
or the batsman is out obstructing the field
or the batsman/striker is out obstructing a ball from being caught
or the batsman is out run out
or the batsman is out stumped
or the batsman is out from a no-ball
or the batsman is out from a wide
then
inform 1 the batsman is out

out bowled
if
atleast 1 of
the wicket is bowled down even if the ball first touches the bat
or the wicket is bowled down even if the ball first touches the batsman
or the batsman breaks his wicket by hitting the ball onto it before the completion of a stroke
or the batsman breaks his wicket by kicking the ball onto it before the completion of a stroke
or the batsman breaks his wicket as a result of attempting to guard his wicket
then
inform 2 the batsman/striker is out bowled

deflected out bowled
if
the ball is deflected on to his wicket
and a decision against him would be justified under the lbw law
then
inform 2 the batsman/striker is out bowled

out time out
if
the incoming batsman wilfully takes more than two minutes to come in
then
inform 2 the batsman is out timed out by the umpire at the bowler's end

out caught
if
the ball touches the batsman's bat
or the ball touches the batsman's hand/glove, holding the bat, below the wrist
and the ball is subsequently held by a fieldsman before it touches the ground
and the catch is fair
then
inform 2 the batsman/striker is out caught

a fair catch
if
atleast 1 of
the fieldsman is within the field of play throughout the act of making a catch
or the ball is hugged to the body of the catcher
or the ball accidentally lodges in the catcher's dress
or the ball accidentally lodges in the wicket-keeper's pads
or not the ball lodges in a protective helmet worn by a fieldsman
or the ball does not touch the ground even though a hand holding it does so in effecting the catch
then
inform 2 the catch is fair

lawful catch
if
a fieldsman catches the ball after it has been lawfully played a second time by the batsman/striker
and the ball has not touched the ground since being first struck
then
inform 2 the catch is fair

touch before
if
atleast 1 of
a fieldsman catches the ball after it has touched the umpire
or a fieldsman catches the ball after it has touched another fieldsman
or a fieldsman catches the ball after it has touched the other batsman
or not the ball has been caught after touching a protective helmet worn by a fieldsman
then
inform 2 the catch is fair

off obstruction
if
the ball is caught off an obstruction within the boundary
and not it has been agreed to regard the obstruction as a boundary
then
inform 2 the catch is fair

act of making a catch
if
the fieldsman first handles the ball
the fieldsman retains complete control over the further disposal of the ball
and the fieldsman remains in the field of play
then
inform 2 the fieldsman is within the field of play throughout the act of making the catch

field of play
if
not the fieldsman may touch any part of his person on the boundary line
or not the fieldsman may touch any part of his person over the boundary line
or not the fieldsman may ground any part of his person on the boundary line
or not the fieldsman may ground any part of his person over the boundary line
then
inform 2 the fieldsman remains in the field of play

out handled the ball
if
either batsman wilfully touches the ball while in play with the other hand
and the other hand is holding the bat
and the ball was handled without the consent of the opposite side
and an appeal has been made by the opposite side
then
inform 2 the batsman is out handled the ball

out hit the ball twice
if
the ball is struck
or the ball is stopped by any part of the batsman
and he wilfully strikes it again with his bat except for the sole purpose of
  guarding his wicket
or he wilfully strikes it again with his person except for the sole purpose of
  guarding his wicket
and an appeal has been made by the opposite side
then
inform 2 the batsman is out hit the ball twice

out returning the ball to a fieldsman
if
the batsman/striker uses his bat to return the ball to any of the fielding side
or the batsman/striker uses his person to return the ball to any of the fielding
  side
and the ball was returned without the consent of the opposite side
and an appeal has been made by the opposite side
then
inform 2 the batsman is out returning the ball to a fieldsman

out hit wicket
if
the ball is in play
and the batsman's wicket is broken with his person
or the batsman's wicket is broken with his dress
or the batsman's wicket is broken with his equipment
and this is the result of any action taken by him in preparing to receive a delivery
or this is the result of action taken by him in receiving a delivery
or this is the result of action taken by him in setting off for his first run immediately after playing at the ball
or this is the result of any action taken by him in setting off for his first run immediately after playing the ball
then
inform 2 the batsman is out hit wicket

hit wicket by guarding wicket
if
the batsman hits down his wicket
and the batsman was lawfully making a second stroke for the purpose of guarding his wicket
and the batsman was doing this within the provisions of the law hit the ball twice
then
inform 2 the batsman is out hit wicket

out lbw
if
the facts for the batsman attempting to play the ball apply
or the facts for the batsman making no attempt to play the ball apply
then
inform 2 the batsman is out lbw

batsman attempting to play the ball
if
the batsman first intercepts with any part of his person a fair ball
or the batsman first intercepts with any part of his dress a fair ball
or the batsman first intercepts with any part of his equipment a fair ball
and the ball would have hit the wicket
and not the ball previously touched his bat
and not the ball previously touched his hand holding the bat
and the additional requirements for where the ball pitched apply
then
inform 2 the facts for the batsman attempting to play the ball apply

batsman making no attempt to play the ball
if
the ball is intercepted outside the line of the off stump
and in the opinion of the umpire, the batsman has made no genuine attempt to play the ball with his bat
and he has intercepted the ball with some part of his person
and the additional requirements for where the ball pitched apply
then
inform 2 the facts for the batsman making no attempt to play the ball apply

where the ball pitched
if
the ball pitched in a straight line between the two wickets
or the ball pitched on the off side of the striker's wicket
or in the case of a ball intercepted full pitch would have pitched in a straight line between the two wickets
and the point of impact is in a straight line between the two wickets, even if above the level of the bails
then
inform 2 the additional requirements for where the ball pitched apply

wilful obstruction
if
either the batsman wilfully obstructs the opposite side by word
or either batsman wilfully obstructs the opposite side by action
and an appeal has been made by the opposite side
then
inform 2 the batsman is out obstructing the field

obstructing a ball from being caught
if
either batsman wilfully causes an obstruction by preventing a catch being made
and an appeal has been made by the opposite side
or the batsman causes the obstruction even though lawfully guarding his wicket under the law hit the ball twice
then
inform 2 the batsman/striker is out obstructing a ball from being caught

out run out
if
either batsman is out of his ground whilst running
or either batsman is out of his ground at any time while the ball is in play
and his wicket is put down by the opposite side
then
inform 2 the batsman is out run out

run out of a no-ball
if
a no-ball has been called
and the striker attempts to run
and the run out facts apply
then
inform 2 the batsman is out run out

out stumped
if
the batsman is receiving the ball
and not the ball is a no-ball
and the batsman is out of his ground otherwise than in attempting a run
and the wicket is put down by the wicket-keeper without the intervention of another fieldsman
then
inform 2 the batsman is out stumped

out from a no-ball
if
the ball is a no-ball
and the batsman breaks the hit the ball twice law
or the batsman breaks the handled the ball law
or the batsman breaks the obstructing the field law
or either batsman is run out
then
inform 2 the batsman is out from a no-ball

out from a wide
if
the ball is a wide-ball
and the batsman breaks the hit wicket law
or the batsman breaks the stumped law
or the batsman breaks the handled the ball law
or the batsman breaks the obstructing the field law
or either batsman is run out
then
inform 2 the batsman is out from a wide

Appendix II - The LISP Expert System

This appendix documents the LISP Expert System. The system is broken up into four files, WINDOW.LSP, which is a general purpose window manager, DATA.LSP which contains the lists of conflicts, opposites etc. KNOW.LSP contains the rules and EXPERT.LSP contains the functions of the expert system.

WINDOW.LSP

```
(DEFUN WINDOW (X1 Y1 X2 Y2)
 (MAKE-WINDOW X1 Y1 X2 Y2) (CLEAR-SCREEN)
 (PRINC (ASCII 218))
 (SETQ A Y2)
 (LOOP
   (PRINC (ASCII 196))
   (SETQ A (- A 1))
   ((EQL A 2) (SETQ A 'A)))
 (PRINC (ASCII 191))
 (SETQ R (ROW))
 (LOOP
   (PRINC (ASCII 179))
   (SET-CURSOR R (- Y2 1))
   (PRINC (ASCII 179))
   (SETQ R (+ R 1))
   ((EQL R (- X2 2)) (SETQ R 'R)))
 (PRINC (ASCII 192))
 (SETQ A Y2)
 (LOOP
   (PRINC (ASCII 196))
   (SETQ A (- A 1))
   ((EQL A 2)(SETQ A 'A)))
 (PRINC (ASCII 217))
 (SET-CURSOR (- X2 2) 0) (INSERT-LINES 1)
 (PRINC (ASCII 179)) (SET-CURSOR (- X2 2) (- Y2 1)) (PRINC (ASCII
179))
 (SETQ X1 (+ X1 1)) (SETQ X2 (- X2 2)) (SETQ Y1 (+ Y1 1)) (SETQ Y2 (-
Y2 2))
 (MAKE-WINDOW X1 Y1 X2 Y2))
```

DATA.LSP

```
(SETQ STATEMENTS '((ANIMAL GIVES MILK)
          (ANIMAL CAN FLY)
          (ANIMAL LAYS EGGS)
          (ANIMAL EATS MEAT)
          (ANIMAL CHEWS CUD)
          (ANIMAL CAN SWIM)
          (ANIMAL FLIES WELL)
          (ANIMAL DOES NOT GIVE MILK)
          (ANIMAL CAN NOT FLY)
          (ANIMAL DOES NOT LAY EGGS)
          (ANIMAL DOES NOT EAT MEAT)
          (ANIMAL DOES NOT CHEW CUD)
          (ANIMAL CAN NOT SWIM)
          (ANIMAL DOES NOT FLY WELL)))

(SETQ IS-LIST '((ANIMAL IS ALBATROSS)
        (ANIMAL IS PENGUIN)
        (ANIMAL IS OSTRICH)
        (ANIMAL IS ZEBRA)
        (ANIMAL IS GIRAFFE)
        (ANIMAL IS TIGER)
        (ANIMAL IS CHEETAH)
        (ANIMAL IS CARNIVORE)
        (ANIMAL IS UNGULATE)
        (ANIMAL IS MAMMAL)
        (ANIMAL IS BIRD)
        (COLOR OF ANIMAL IS TAWNY)
        (COLOR OF ANIMAL IS BLACK AND WHITE)))

(SETQ HAS-LIST '((ANIMAL HAS HAIR)
        (ANIMAL HAS FEATHERS)
        (ANIMAL HAS POINTED TEETH)
        (ANIMAL HAS CLAWS)
        (ANIMAL HAS FORWARD EYES)
        (ANIMAL HAS HOOFS)
        (ANIMAL HAS DARK SPOTS)
        (ANIMAL HAS BLACK STRIPES)
```

```
        (ANIMAL HAS LONG NECK)
        (ANIMAL HAS LONG LEGS)))

(SETQ CONFLICTS '((ANIMAL IS UNGULATE CARNIVORE)
        (ANIMAL IS BIRD MAMMAL)
        (ANIMAL HAS HAIR FEATHERS)
        (ANIMAL HAS HOOFS CLAWS)
        (ANIMAL HAS (DARK SPOTS)(BLACK STRIPES))
        (COLOR OF ANIMAL  IS TAWNY (BLACK AND WHITE))))

(SETQ OPPOSITES '(((ANIMAL GIVES MILK) OPP (ANIMAL DOES
NOT GIVE MILK))
        ((ANIMAL CAN FLY) OPP (ANIMAL CAN NOT FLY))
        ((ANIMAL LAYS EGGS) OPP (ANIMAL DOES NOT LAY
EGGS))
        ((ANIMAL EATS MEAT) OPP (ANIMAL DOES NOT EAT
MEAT))
        ((ANIMAL CHEWS CUD) OPP (ANIMAL DOES NOT CHEW
CUD))
        ((ANIMAL CAN SWIM) OPP (ANIMAL CAN NOT SWIM))
        ((ANIMAL FLIES WELL) OPP (ANIMAL DOES NOT FLY
WELL))))
```

KNOW.LSP

```
(SETQ HYPOTHESES '((ANIMAL IS ALBATROSS)
        (ANIMAL IS PENGUIN)
        (ANIMAL IS OSTRICH)
        (ANIMAL IS ZEBRA)
        (ANIMAL IS GIRAFFE)
        (ANIMAL IS TIGER)
        (ANIMAL IS CHEETAH)))
(SETQ RULES '(

(IDENTIFY1
   (IF (ANIMAL HAS HAIR))
   (THEN (ANIMAL IS MAMMAL)))
```

```
(IDENTIFY2
   (IF (ANIMAL GIVES MILK))
   (THEN (ANIMAL IS MAMMAL)))

(IDENTIFY3
   (IF (ANIMAL HAS FEATHERS))
   (THEN (ANIMAL IS BIRD)))

(IDENTIFY4
   (IF (ANIMAL CAN FLY)
     (ANIMAL LAYS EGGS))
   (THEN (ANIMAL IS BIRD)))

(IDENTIFY5
   (IF (ANIMAL EATS MEAT))
   (THEN (ANIMAL IS CARNIVORE)))

(IDENTIFY6
   (IF (ANIMAL HAS POINTED TEETH)
     (ANIMAL HAS CLAWS)
     (ANIMAL HAS FORWARD EYES))
   (THEN (ANIMAL IS CARNIVORE)))

(IDENTIFY7
   (IF (ANIMAL IS MAMMAL)
     (ANIMAL HAS HOOFS))
   (THEN (ANIMAL IS UNGULATE)))

(IDENTIFY8
   (IF (ANIMAL IS MAMMAL)
     (ANIMAL CHEWS CUD))
   (THEN (ANIMAL IS UNGULATE)
      (ANIMAL IS EVEN TOED)))
```

```
(IDENTIFY9
  (IF (ANIMAL IS MAMMAL)
    (ANIMAL IS CARNIVORE)
    (COLOR OF ANIMAL IS TAWNY)
    (ANIMAL HAS DARK SPOTS))
  (THEN (ANIMAL IS CHEETAH)))

(IDENTIFY10
  (IF (ANIMAL IS MAMMAL)
    (ANIMAL IS CARNIVORE)
    (COLOR OF ANIMAL IS TAWNY)
    (ANIMAL HAS BLACK STRIPES))
  (THEN (ANIMAL IS TIGER)))

(IDENTIFY11
  (IF (ANIMAL IS UNGULATE)
    (ANIMAL HAS LONG NECK)
    (ANIMAL HAS LONG LEGS)
    (ANIMAL HAS DARK SPOTS))
  (THEN (ANIMAL IS GIRAFFE)))

(IDENTIFY12
  (IF (ANIMAL IS UNGULATE)
    (ANIMAL HAS BLACK STRIPES))
  (THEN (ANIMAL IS ZEBRA)))

(IDENTIFY13
  (IF (ANIMAL IS BIRD)
    (ANIMAL CAN NOT FLY)
    (ANIMAL HAS LONG NECK)
    (ANIMAL HAS LONG LEGS)
    (COLOR OF ANIMAL IS BLACK AND WHITE))
  (THEN (ANIMAL IS OSTRICH)))
```

```
(IDENTIFY14
   (IF (ANIMAL IS BIRD)
     (ANIMAL CAN NOT FLY)
     (ANIMAL CAN SWIM)
     (COLOR OF ANIMAL IS BLACK AND WHITE))
   (THEN (ANIMAL IS PENGUIN)))

(IDENTIFY15
   (IF (ANIMAL IS BIRD)
     (ANIMAL FLIES WELL))
   (THEN (ANIMAL IS ALBATROSS)))   ))
```

EXPERT.LSP

```
(DEFUN EXPERT-SYSTEMS (ASKED FACTS A)
 (LOOP
  (MAKE-WINDOW 0 0 25 80) (CLEAR-SCREEN) (WINDOW 0 0 9 60)
  (SETQ ASKED NIL) (SETQ FACTS NIL) (CLEAR-SCREEN)
  (PRINC "            EXPERT SYSTEMS OPTIONS MENU       ")
(TERPRI)
  (PRINC "            -----------------------------     ") (TERPRI)
  (PRINC "PRESS <SPACE BAR> TO ESCAPE") (TERPRI)
  (PRINC "1") (PRINC " - OUTPUT DATA BASE AND KNOWLEDGE
BASE") (TERPRI)
  (PRINC "2") (PRINC " - FORWARD CHAINING") (TERPRI)
  (PRINC "3") (PRINC " - BACKWARD CHAINING") (TERPRI) (PRINC
"= = > ")
  (LOOP
   (SETQ A (READ-BYTE))
   ((EQL A 32) (MAKE-WINDOW 0 0 25 80) (CLEAR-SCREEN)
(RETURN))
   ((OR (EQL A 49) (EQL A 50) (EQL A 51)) (PRINC (- A 48))))
  (TONE 30000 2000)
  (COND
   ((EQL A 49) (CATCH NIL (VALIDATION)))
   ((EQL A 50) (CATCH NIL (FORWARD-CHAINING)))
   ((EQL A 51) (CATCH NIL (BACKWARD-CHAINING))))
  (MAKE-WINDOW 0 0 25 80) (CLEAR-SCREEN) (WINDOW 5 10 4 60)
  (PRINC "WOULD YOU LIKE TO SEE THE MAIN MENU AGAIN
```

```
(Y/N)?")
  (LOOP
   (SETQ A (READ-BYTE))
   ((OR (EQL A 110) (EQL A 78)) (PRINC (ASCII A)) (TONE 30000 2000)
    (MAKE-WINDOW 0 0 25 80) (CLEAR-SCREEN) (RETURN))
   ((OR (EQL A 121) (EQL A 89)) (PRINC (ASCII A)) (TONE 30000 2000)
    (MAKE-WINDOW 0 0 25 80) (CLEAR-SCREEN)))))

(DEFUN VALIDATION (A)
 (LOOP
  (MAKE-WINDOW 0 0 25 80) (CLEAR-SCREEN) (WINDOW 0 0 9 65)
  (PRINC "              OUTPUT MENU              ") (TERPRI)
  (PRINC "              -------------        ") (TERPRI)
  (PRINC "PRESS THE NUMBER CORRESPONDING TO THE BLOCK
YOU WANT DISPLAYED")
  (TERPRI) (PRINC "PRESS <SPACE BAR> TO ESCAPE") (TERPRI)
  (PRINC "1") (PRINC " - DATA BASE") (TERPRI 1)
  (PRINC "2") (PRINC " - KNOWLEDGE BASE") (TERPRI 1) (PRINC
"= = > ")
  (LOOP
   (SETQ A (READ-BYTE))
   ((EQL A 32) (MAKE-WINDOW 0 0 25 80) (CLEAR-SCREEN)
 (RETURN NIL))
   ((OR (EQL A 49) (EQL A 50)) (PRINC (- A 48))))
  (TONE 30000 2000) (CLEAR-SCREEN)
  (COND
   ((EQL A 49) (CATCH NIL (OUTPUT-DATA-MEMORY)))
   ((EQL A 50) (CATCH NIL (OUTPUT-KNOWLEDGE-BASE))))))

(DEFUN OUTPUT-KNOWLEDGE-BASE (A)
 (LOOP
  (MAKE-WINDOW 0 0 25 80) (CLEAR-SCREEN) (WINDOW 0 0 9 67)
  (PRINC "         KNOWLEDGE BASE OUTPUT MENU ") (TERPRI)
  (PRINC "         ----------------------------") (TERPRI)
  (PRINC "PRESS THE NUMBER CORRESPONDING TO THE BLOCK
YOU WANT DISPLAYED")
  (TERPRI) (PRINC "PRESS <SPACE BAR> TO RETURN TO MAIN
OUTPUT MENU") (TERPRI)
  (PRINC "1") (PRINC " - HYPOTHESES") (TERPRI)
```

```
  (PRINC "2") (PRINC " - PRODUCTION RULES") (TERPRI) (PRINC
"= = > ")
  (LOOP
   (SETQ A (READ-BYTE))
   ((EQL A 32) (MAKE-WINDOW 0 0 25 80) (CLEAR-SCREEN)
(RETURN NIL))
   ((OR (EQL A 49) (EQL A 50)) (PRINC (- A 48))))
  (TONE 30000 2000)
  (COND
   ((EQL A 49) (MAKE-WINDOW 0 0 25 80) (CLEAR-SCREEN)
(WINDOW 0 0 25 40)
    (PRINC "*** HYPOTHESES ***") (HELP-PRINT HYPOTHESES)
(TERPRI)
    (PRINC "PRESS ANY KEY WHEN READY") (READ-BYTE))
   ((EQL A 50) (MAKE-WINDOW 0 0 25 80) (CLEAR-SCREEN)
(WINDOW 0 0 25 50)
    (PRINC "*** PRODUCTION RULES ***") (OUTPUT-RULES
RULES) (TERPRI)
    (PRINC "PRESS ANY KEY WHEN READY") (READ-BYTE)))))

(DEFUN OUTPUT-DATA-MEMORY ()
 (LOOP
  (MAKE-WINDOW 0 0 25 80) (CLEAR-SCREEN) (WINDOW 0 0 12 65)
  (PRINC "          DATA MEMORY OUTPUT MENU ") (TERPRI)
  (PRINC "          ------------------------- ") (TERPRI)
  (PRINC "PRESS THE NUMBER CORRESPONDING TO THE BLOCK
YOU WANT DISPLAYED")
  (TERPRI) (PRINC "PRESS <SPACE BAR> TO RETURN TO MAIN
OUTPUT MENU") (TERPRI)
  (PRINC "1") (PRINC " - UNSTRUCTURED STATEMENTS") (TERPRI
1)
  (PRINC "2") (PRINC " - IS-ARE RELATIONS") (TERPRI 1)
  (PRINC "3") (PRINC " - HAS-HAVE RELATIONS") (TERPRI 1)
  (PRINC "4") (PRINC " - CONFLICTS") (TERPRI 1)
  (PRINC "5") (PRINC " - OPPOSITES") (TERPRI 1) (PRINC "= = > ")
  (LOOP
   (SETQ A (READ-BYTE))
   ((EQL A 32) (MAKE-WINDOW 0 0 25 80) (CLEAR-SCREEN)
(RETURN NIL))
```

```
  ((AND (> A 48) (< A 54)) (PRINC (- A 48))))
  (TONE 30000 2000)
  (COND
  ((EQL A 49) (MAKE-WINDOW 0 0 25 80) (CLEAR-SCREEN)
(WINDOW 0 0 25 40)
   (PRINC "*** STATEMENTS ***") (HELP-PRINT STATEMENTS)
(TERPRI)
   (PRINC "PRESS ANY KEY WHEN READY") (READ-BYTE))
  ((EQL A 50) (MAKE-WINDOW 0 0 25 80) (CLEAR-SCREEN)
(WINDOW 0 0 25 40)
   (PRINC "*** IS-ARE RELATIONS ***") (HELP-PRINT IS-LIST)
(TERPRI)
   (PRINC "PRESS ANY KEY WHEN READY") (READ-BYTE))
  ((EQL A 51) (MAKE-WINDOW 0 0 25 80) (CLEAR-SCREEN)
(WINDOW 0 0 25 40)
   (PRINC "*** HAS-HAVE RELATIONS ***") (HELP-PRINT HAS-
LIST) (TERPRI)
   (PRINC "PRESS ANY KEY WHEN READY") (READ-BYTE))
  ((EQL A 52) (MAKE-WINDOW 0 0 25 80) (CLEAR-SCREEN)
(WINDOW 0 0 25 50)
   (PRINC "*** CONFLICTS ***") (OUTPUT-CONFS-AND-OPPS
CONFLICTS) (TERPRI)
   (PRINC "PRESS ANY KEY WHEN READY") (READ-BYTE))
  ((EQL A 53) (MAKE-WINDOW 0 0 25 80) (CLEAR-SCREEN)
(WINDOW 0 0 25 55)
   (PRINC "*** OPPOSITES ***") (OUTPUT-CONFS-AND-OPPS
OPPOSITES) (TERPRI)
   (PRINC "PRESS ANY KEY WHEN READY") (READ-BYTE)))))

(DEFUN OUTPUT-RULES (TEMP-RULES LST L)
 (TERPRI)
 (LOOP
  ((NULL TEMP-RULES))
  (PRINC (CAAR TEMP-RULES)) (TERPRI)
  (SETQ LST (CDAR TEMP-RULES))
  (LOOP
   ((NULL LST))
   (SETQ L (CAR LST))
   (LOOP
```

```
  ((NULL L))
  (COND
   ((ATOM (CAR L)) (PRINC (CAR L)))
   (T (PRINTING (CAR L))))
  (TERPRI)
  (SETQ L (CDR L)))
 (SETQ LST (CDR LST)))
 (TERPRI 1) (TONE 30000 5000)
 (SETQ TEMP-RULES (CDR TEMP-RULES))))

(DEFUN OUTPUT-CONFS-AND-OPPS (LST L MARK REL)
 (TERPRI)
 (LOOP
  ((NULL LST))
  (SETQ L (CAR LST) REL NIL MARK NIL)
  (LOOP
   ((NULL L))
   (COND ((AND (NOT (EQL REL NIL)) (NOT (EQL REL MARK)))
(PRINC ",")))
   (COND ((OR (EQL (CAR L) 'IS) (EQL (CAR L) 'ARE) (EQL (CAR L)
'HAS)
      (EQL (CAR L) 'HAVE)) (SETQ REL (CAR L))))
   (COND ((ATOM (CAR L)) (PRINC (CAR L)) (PRINC " "))
     (T (PRINTING (CAR L)) (PRINC " ")))
   (SETQ MARK (CAR L))
   (SETQ L (CDR L)))
  (TERPRI)
  (SETQ LST (CDR LST))))

(DEFUN GET-THEN-PART (RULE)
 (CDR (ASSOC 'THEN RULE)))

(DEFUN CHECK-THEN-PART (IF-PART RULES)
 (LOOP
  ((NULL RULES) NIL)
  ((MEMBER IF-PART (GET-THEN-PART (CAR RULES)) 'EQUAL) T)
  (SETQ RULES (CDR RULES))))
```

```
(DEFUN GET-IF-PART (RULE)
 (CDR (ASSOC 'IF RULE)))

(DEFUN CHECK-IF-PART (IF-PARTS RULES)
 (COND
  ((NULL IF-PARTS) NIL)
  ((CHECK-THEN-PART (CAR IF-PARTS) RULES)(CHECK-IF-PART
(CDR IF-PARTS) RULES))
  (T (CONS (CAR IF-PARTS) (CHECK-IF-PART (CDR IF-PARTS)
RULES)))))

(DEFUN EXPAND-LIST (LST1 LST2)
  (COND
   ((NULL LST1) LST2)
   ((MEMBER (CAR LST1) LST2 'EQUAL) (EXPAND-LIST (CDR LST1)
LST2))
   (T (EXPAND-LIST (CDR LST1) (APPEND LST2 (LIST (CAR
LST1)))))))

(DEFUN COLLECT-POSSIBLES (RULES RLS)
 (SETQ POSSIBLES NIL RLS RULES)
 (LOOP
  ((NULL RLS))
  (SETQ POSSIBLES
    (EXPAND-LIST (CHECK-IF-PART (GET-IF-PART (CAR RLS))
RULES) POSSIBLES))
  (SETQ RLS (CDR RLS))))

(DEFUN HELP-PRINT (LST A)
  (COND
   ((NULL LST) (PRINC " NIL") (TERPRI))
   (T (TERPRI)
     (LOOP
      ((NULL LST))
      (SETQ A (CAR LST))
      (LOOP
      ((NULL A))
      (PRINC (CAR A))
      (PRINC " ")
```

```
    (SETQ A (CDR A)))
    (TERPRI)
    (SETQ LST (CDR LST))))))

(DEFUN PRINTING (LST)
 (LOOP
  ((NULL LST))
  (PRINC (CAR LST))
  (COND ((NOT (NULL (CDR LST))) (PRINC " ")))
  (SETQ LST (CDR LST))))

(DEFUN CURRENT-EXPLANATION (RULE FACT-LIST IF-PART LST1
LST2)
 (PRINC "?") (TONE 30000 1000) (WINDOW 5 15 15 51) (CLEAR-
SCREEN)
 (PRINC "PRESS ANY KEY TO RESUME CHAINING") (TERPRI)
(PRINC "RULE:")
 (PRINC (CAR RULE)) (TERPRI) (SETQ IF-PART (GET-IF-PART
RULE))
 (PRINC "FACTS TO BE INFERED BY THIS RULE:") (HELP-PRINT
(GET-THEN-PART RULE))
 (LOOP
  ((NULL IF-PART))
  (COND ((MEMBER (CAR IF-PART) FACT-LIST 'EQUAL)
     (SETQ LST1 (APPEND LST1 (LIST (CAR IF-PART)))))
    (T (SETQ LST2 (APPEND LST2 (LIST (CAR IF-PART))))))
  (SETQ IF-PART (CDR IF-PART)))
 (PRINC "FACTS CONFIRMED AT THE CURRENT RULE:") (HELP-
PRINT LST1)
 (PRINC "FACTS REQUIRED TO BE CONFIRMED:") (HELP-PRINT
LST2)
 (READ-BYTE) (MAKE-WINDOW 0 0 20 80) (CLEAR-SCREEN)
(WINDOW 0 0 21 51)
 (WINDOW 0 51 25 29) (CLEAR-SCREEN)
 (COND ((NOT (NULL FACTS)) (PRINC "     FACTS") (TERPRI)
    (PRINC "     -----") (HELP-PRINT FACTS))))
```

```
(DEFUN FIND-OPPOSITES (A LST)
 (COND
  ((NULL LST) NIL)
  ((EQUAL A (CAAR LST)) (CADDAR LST))
  ((EQUAL A (CADDAR LST)) (CAAR LST))
  (T (FIND-OPPOSITES A (CDR LST)))))

(DEFUN ACCESS-CONFLICT-VALUES (LST1 LST2 CONFLIST)
 (LOOP
  ((NULL LST2) NIL)
  ((OR (EQUAL LST1 (CAR LST2)) (EQUAL LST1 (LIST (CAR LST2))))
   (SETQ CONFLIST (EXPAND-LIST (CDR LST2) CONFLIST)))
  (SETQ CONFLIST (APPEND CONFLIST (LIST (CAR LST2))) LST2
(CDR LST2))))

(DEFUN HELP-FIND-CONFLICTS (A LST)
 (COND
  ((AND (EQL (CAR A) (CAR LST)) (OR (EQL (CAR A) 'IS) (EQL (CAR
A) 'ARE)
                    (EQL (CAR A) 'HAS) (EQL (CAR A) 'HAVE)))
   (ACCESS-CONFLICT-VALUES (CDR A) (CDR LST)))
  ((EQL (CAR A) (CAR LST)) (HELP-FIND-CONFLICTS (CDR A) (CDR
LST)))
  (T NIL)))

(DEFUN RETURN-CONFLICTS (C C-LIST LST LST1)
 (LOOP
  (SETQ LST (APPEND LST (LIST (CAR C))))
  ((OR (EQL (CAR C) 'IS) (EQL (CAR C) 'ARE)
    (EQL (CAR C) 'HAS) (EQL (CAR C) 'HAVE)))
  (SETQ C (CDR C)))
 (LOOP
  ((NULL C-LIST) LST1)
  (COND
   ((ATOM (CAR C-LIST))
    (SETQ LST1 (CONS (APPEND LST (LIST (CAR C-LIST))) LST1)))
   (T (SETQ LST1 (CONS (APPEND LST (CAR C-LIST)) LST1))))
  (SETQ C-LIST (CDR C-LIST))))
```

```
(DEFUN FIND-CONFLICTS (A CONFL LST)
 (LOOP
  ((NULL CONFL) NIL)
  (SETQ LST (HELP-FIND-CONFLICTS A (CAR CONFL)))
  ((NOT (NULL LST)) (RETURN-CONFLICTS A LST))
  (SETQ CONFL (CDR CONFL))))

(DEFUN ASK-STATEMENT (IF-PART RULE A)
 (LOOP
  (MAKE-WINDOW 1 1 18 49) (CLEAR-SCREEN) (PRINC "PRESS  ?
FOR EXPLANATION")
  (TERPRI) (PRINTING IF-PART) (PRINC " (Y/N)? ")
  (LOOP
   (SETQ A (READ-BYTE))
   ((EQL A 63) (CURRENT-EXPLANATION RULE FACTS))
   ((OR (EQL A 89) (EQL A 121)) (SETQ A 'Y))
   ((OR (EQL A 110) (EQL A 78)) (SETQ A 'N)))
  ((OR (EQL A 'Y) (EQL A 'N))))
 (PRINC A) (TONE 30000 2000)
 (COND
  ((EQL A 'Y) (PROGN
   (COND ((NOT (MEMBER IF-PART FACTS 'EQUAL))
    (SETQ FACTS (APPEND FACTS (LIST IF-PART)))))
   (COND ((NOT (MEMBER (FIND-OPPOSITES IF-PART OPPOSITES)
ASKED 'EQUAL))
    (SETQ ASKED (APPEND ASKED (LIST (FIND-OPPOSITES IF-PART
OPPOSITES))))))))
  ((EQL A 'N) (PROGN
   (COND ((NOT (MEMBER IF-PART ASKED 'EQUAL))
    (SETQ ASKED (APPEND ASKED (LIST IF-PART)))))
   (COND ((NOT (MEMBER (FIND-OPPOSITES IF-PART OPPOSITES)
FACTS 'EQUAL))
    (SETQ FACTS (APPEND FACTS (LIST (FIND-OPPOSITES IF-PART
OPPOSITES)))))))))
 (MAKE-WINDOW 1 52 23 27) (CLEAR-SCREEN) (PRINC "
FACTS") (TERPRI)
 (PRINC "    -----") (HELP-PRINT FACTS)
 (COND
  ((EQL A 'Y) T)
```

```
 ((EQL A 'N) NIL)))

(DEFUN CHECK-RELATION (LST1 LST2)
 (COND
   ((AND (EQL (CAR LST1) (CAR LST2)) (OR (EQL (CAR LST1) 'IS)
    (EQL (CAR LST1) 'ARE) (EQL (CAR LST1) 'HAS) (EQL (CAR
LST1) 'HAVE))))
   ((EQL (CAR LST1) (CAR LST2)) (CHECK-RELATION (CDR LST1)
(CDR LST2)))
   (T NIL)))

(DEFUN PRINT-RELATION (LST PART)
 (LOOP
  (SETQ PART (APPEND PART (LIST (CAR LST))))
  ((OR (EQL (CAR LST) 'IS) (EQL (CAR LST) 'ARE) (EQL (CAR LST)
'HAS)
    (EQL (CAR LST) 'HAVE)) (PRINTING PART))
  (SETQ LST (CDR LST)))
 (PRINC ":-"))

(DEFUN PRINT-VALUES (LST REST)
 (LOOP
  (SETQ REST (CONS (CAR LST) REST))
  ((OR (EQL (CAR LST) 'IS) (EQL (CAR LST) 'ARE) (EQL (CAR LST)
'HAS)
    (EQL (CAR LST) 'HAVE)) (PRINTING (CDR LST)))
  (SETQ LST (CDR LST))))

(DEFUN READING (NUM A SUM DEC LST)
 (SETQ SUM 0 DEC 1)
 (LOOP
  (SETQ A (READ-BYTE))
  ((EQL A 63) ?)
  ((EQL A 32)
   (COND
   ((NULL LST) | |)
   (T (LOOP
     ((NULL LST) SUM)
     (SETQ SUM (+ SUM (* (CAR LST) DEC)))
```

```
    (SETQ DEC (* DEC 10))
    (SETQ LST (CDR LST))))))
  (COND
   ((AND (NULL LST) (EQL A 48)))
   ((AND (> A 47) (< A 58))
    (SETQ LST (CONS (- A 48) LST)) (PRINC (ASCII A))))))

(DEFUN ASK-THE-USER (IF-PART RULE)
  (COND
    ((MEMBER IF-PART STATEMENTS 'EQUAL) (ASK-STATEMENT
IF-PART RULE))
    (T (ASK-RELATION IF-PART RULE))))

(DEFUN ADD-THEN-PARTS (LISTHEAD RULE TEMP CONF)
  (SETQ TEMP (GET-THEN-PART RULE))
  (COND
    ((STRING= LISTHEAD 'FACTS)
     (SETQ FACTS (EXPAND-LIST TEMP FACTS))
     (LOOP
     ((NULL TEMP) NIL)
     (SETQ CONF (FIND-CONFLICTS (CAR TEMP) CONFLICTS))
     (SETQ ASKED (EXPAND-LIST CONF ASKED))
     (SETQ TEMP (CDR TEMP))))
    ((STRING= LISTHEAD 'ASKED) (SETQ ASKED (EXPAND-LIST
TEMP ASKED)))))

(DEFUN CONCLUDE (A)
  (PRINC A) (TONE 30000 1000) (MAKE-WINDOW 0 0 25 80) (CLEAR-
SCREEN)
  (WINDOW 0 15 25 50) (PRINC "                FACTS") (TERPRI 1)
  (PRINC "              -----") (HELP-PRINT FACTS) (TERPRI 2)
  (PRINC "PRESS ANY KEY TO RETURN BACK TO MAIN MENU")
(READ-BYTE)
  (MAKE-WINDOW 0 0 25 80) (CLEAR-SCREEN))

(DEFUN ASK-RELATION (IF-PART RULE LST REL COUNT TEMP A
R C)
  (SETQ LST (GET-IF-PART RULE))
  (LOOP
```

```
  ((NULL LST) NIL)
  (COND ((CHECK-RELATION IF-PART (CAR LST))
      (SETQ REL (APPEND REL (LIST (CAR LST))))))
  (SETQ LST (CDR LST)))
 (LOOP
  (MAKE-WINDOW 1 1 18 49) (CLEAR-SCREEN) (SETQ COUNT 0
TEMP REL)
  (CLEAR-SCREEN) (PRINC "PRESS ? FOR EXPLANATION")
(TERPRI 1)
  (PRINC "ENTER YOUR CHOICE (NUMBER) AND PRESS <SPACE
BAR>") (TERPRI 1)
  (PRINC "PRESS <SPACE BAR> TO REJECT THE VALUES ON VDU")
(TERPRI 1)
  (PRINT-RELATION (CAR TEMP))
  (LOOP
   ((NULL TEMP) NIL)
   (SETQ COUNT (+ COUNT 1))
   (TERPRI 1) (PRINC COUNT) (PRINC " - ")
   (PRINT-VALUES (CAR TEMP))
   (SETQ TEMP (CDR TEMP)))
  (TERPRI 1) (PRINC "= = > ") (SETQ R (ROW) C (COLUMN))
  (LOOP
   (SETQ A (READING))
   ((EQL A '?) (CURRENT-EXPLANATION RULE FACTS))
   ((OR (EQL A | |) (AND (> A 0) (< = A COUNT))))
   (SET-CURSOR R C) (PRINC "            ") (SET-CURSOR R C))
  (COND
   ((NUMBERP A) (PROGN
    (COND ((NOT (MEMBER (NTH (- A 1) REL) FACTS 'EQUAL))
       (SETQ FACTS (CONS (NTH (- A 1) REL) FACTS))
       (MAKE-WINDOW 1 52 23 27) (CLEAR-SCREEN) (PRINC "
FACTS")
       (TERPRI) (PRINC "      -----") (HELP-PRINT FACTS)))
    (SETQ ASKED
       (EXPAND-LIST (FIND-CONFLICTS (NTH (- A 1) REL)
CONFLICTS) ASKED))
    (SETQ REL (DELETE (NTH (- A 1) REL) REL 'EQUAL))))
   ((EQL A | |)
    (SETQ ASKED (EXPAND-LIST REL ASKED))
```

```
    (SETQ REL NIL)))
   ((EQL A | |) NIL)
   ((NULL REL) T)))

(DEFUN COLLECT-RULES (THEN-PART RULE-LIST)
  (COND
   ((NULL RULE-LIST) NIL)
   ((MEMBER THEN-PART (GET-THEN-PART (CAR RULE-LIST))
'EQUAL)
    (CONS (CAR RULE-LIST) (COLLECT-RULES THEN-PART (CDR
RULE-LIST))))
   (T (COLLECT-RULES THEN-PART (CDR RULE-LIST)))))

(DEFUN FORWARD-CHAINING (POSSIBLES TEMP-RULES HYP UP-
TO-NOW EXIT ENTER
IF-PARTS THEN-PARTS H A TCON)
  (COLLECT-POSSIBLES RULES) (MAKE-WINDOW 0 0 25 80) (CLEAR-
SCREEN)
  (WINDOW 0 0 21 51) (WINDOW 21 0 4 51) (WINDOW 0 51 25 29)
  (PRINC "FACTS WILL BE DISPLAYED") (PRINC "HERE DURING
INTERACTION")
  (SETQ TEMP-RULES RULES HYP NIL UP-TO-NOW NIL)
  (LOOP
   ((OR (NULL TEMP-RULES) (EQL HYP T)))
   (SETQ EXIT T ENTER T)
   (SETQ IF-PARTS (GET-IF-PART (CAR TEMP-RULES)))
   (SETQ THEN-PARTS (GET-THEN-PART (CAR TEMP-RULES)))
   (SETQ H THEN-PARTS)
   (LOOP
    ((NULL H))
    ((MEMBER (CAR H) HYPOTHESES 'EQUAL)
     (MAKE-WINDOW 22 1 2 49) (CLEAR-SCREEN) (PRINC
"HYPOTHESIS TO BE PROVED")
     (TERPRI 1) (PRINTING (CAR H)) (TONE 30000 1000))
    (SETQ H (CDR H)))
   (LOOP
    ((NULL THEN-PARTS))
    (SETQ TCON (FIND-CONFLICTS (CAR THEN-PARTS) CONFLICTS))
    (LOOP
```

```
((NULL TCON))
((MEMBER (CAR TCON) FACTS 'EQUAL) (SETQ ENTER NIL))
(SETQ TCON (CDR TCON)))
((EQL ENTER NIL))
(SETQ THEN-PARTS (CDR THEN-PARTS)))
(COND
((EQL ENTER T)
(LOOP
((OR (NULL IF-PARTS) (EQL EXIT NIL)))
((AND (MEMBER (CAR IF-PARTS) ASKED 'EQUAL)
(NOT (MEMBER (CAR IF-PARTS) FACTS 'EQUAL))) (SETQ
EXIT NIL))
(COND
((AND (MEMBER (CAR IF-PARTS) POSSIBLES 'EQUAL)
(NOT (MEMBER (CAR IF-PARTS) FACTS 'EQUAL)))
(SETQ EXIT (ASK-THE-USER (CAR IF-PARTS) (CAR TEMP-
RULES)))))
((AND (MEMBER (CAR IF-PARTS) STATEMENTS 'EQUAL) (EQL
EXIT NIL))
(SETQ EXIT | |))
(SETQ IF-PARTS (CDR IF-PARTS))))
((EQL ENTER NIL) (SETQ EXIT NIL)))
(SETQ THEN-PARTS (GET-THEN-PART (CAR TEMP-RULES)))
(COND
((EQL EXIT NIL) (ADD-THEN-PARTS 'ASKED (CAR TEMP-
RULES)))
((EQL EXIT T) (ADD-THEN-PARTS 'FACTS (CAR TEMP-RULES))
(MAKE-WINDOW 1 52 23 27) (CLEAR-SCREEN) (PRINC "
FACTS")
(TERPRI 1) (PRINC "      -----") (HELP-PRINT FACTS)
(SETQ UP-TO-NOW (EXPAND-LIST THEN-PARTS UP-TO-NOW))))
(LOOP
((NULL THEN-PARTS) NIL)
((AND (MEMBER (CAR THEN-PARTS) HYPOTHESES 'EQUAL)
(MEMBER (CAR THEN-PARTS) FACTS))
(TONE 30000 5000) (MAKE-WINDOW 0 0 25 80) (CLEAR-SCREEN)
(SETQ HYP T)
(WINDOW 9 25 4 30) (PRINTING (CAR THEN-PARTS)) (TONE 30000
4000)
```

```
   (MAKE-WINDOW 0 0 25 80) (CLEAR-SCREEN))
   (SETQ THEN-PARTS (CDR THEN-PARTS)))
  (SETQ TEMP-RULES (CDR TEMP-RULES)))
 (COND
  ((EQL HYP NIL) (MAKE-WINDOW 0 0 25 80) (CLEAR-SCREEN)
(WINDOW 8 15 9 50)
   (PRINC "INSUFFICIENT INFORMATION") (TONE 30000 2000)
(TERPRI 2)
   (PRINC "CONCLUSIONS REACHED:") (HELP-PRINT UP-TO-NOW)
(TONE 30000 5000)
   (MAKE-WINDOW 0 0 25 80) (CLEAR-SCREEN)))
 (WINDOW 0 0 9 60) (PRINC "WOULD YOU LIKE TO SEE THE FACTS
?")
 (LOOP
  (SETQ A (READ-BYTE))
  ((OR (EQL A 121) (EQL A 89)) (CONCLUDE (ASCII A)))
  ((OR (EQL A 110) (EQL A 78)) (PRINC (ASCII A))))
 (TONE 30000 1000) (MAKE-WINDOW 0 0 25 80) (CLEAR-SCREEN))

(DEFUN TRYRULE1 (RULE IF-PARTS ONE)
  (SETQ IF-PARTS (GET-IF-PART RULE))
  (SETQ ONE T)
  (LOOP
   ((NULL IF-PARTS))
   ((NOT (MEMBER (CAR IF-PARTS) FACTS 'EQUAL)) (SETQ ONE
NIL))
   (SETQ IF-PARTS (CDR IF-PARTS)))
  (COND
   ((EQL ONE T) (ADD-THEN-PARTS 'FACTS RULE)
    (MAKE-WINDOW 1 52 23 27) (CLEAR-SCREEN) (PRINC "
FACTS") (TERPRI)
    (PRINC "          -----") (HELP-PRINT FACTS)
    (SETQ UP-TO-NOW (EXPAND-LIST (GET-THEN-PART RULE) UP-
TO-NOW))))
  (COND ((EQL ONE NIL) NIL)
     ((EQL ONE T) T)))

 (DEFUN BACKWARD-CHAINING (HYPO HYP UP-TO-NOW A EXIT)
  (MAKE-WINDOW 0 0 25 80) (CLEAR-SCREEN) (WINDOW 0 0 21 51)
```

```
(WINDOW 21 0 4 51)
 (WINDOW 0 51 25 29) (MAKE-WINDOW 1 52 23 27)
 (PRINC "FACTS WILL BE DISPLAYED") (PRINC "HERE DURING
INTERACTION")
 (TONE 20000 1000) (SETQ HYPO HYPOTHESES) (SETQ HYP NIL UP-
TO-NOW NIL)
 (LOOP
  ((NULL HYPO))
  (MAKE-WINDOW 22 1 2 49) (CLEAR-SCREEN) (PRINC
"HYPOTHESIS TO BE PROVED")
  (TERPRI) (PRINTING (CAR HYPO)) (TONE 30000 2000)
  (SETQ HYP (VERIFY (CAR HYPO)))
  ((EQL HYP T))
  (SETQ HYPO (CDR HYPO)))
 (TONE 30000 5000)
 (COND
  ((EQL HYP T) (MAKE-WINDOW 0 0 25 80) (CLEAR-SCREEN)
(WINDOW 10 25 5 30)
   (PRINTING (CAR HYPO)) (TONE 30000 4000) (MAKE-WINDOW 0 0
25 80)
   (CLEAR-SCREEN))
  ((EQL HYP NIL) (MAKE-WINDOW 0 0 25 80) (CLEAR-SCREEN)
(WINDOW 7 20 10 40)
   (PRINC "INSUFFICIENT INFORMATION") (TONE 30000 2000)
(TERPRI 2)
   (PRINC "CONCLUSIONS REACHED:") (HELP-PRINT UP-TO-NOW)
(TONE 30000 5000)
   (MAKE-WINDOW 0 0 25 80) ((CLEAR-SCREEN))))
 (WINDOW 0 0 9 60) (PRINC "WOULD YOU LIKE TO SEE THE FACTS
(Y/N)?")
 (LOOP
  (SETQ A (READ-BYTE))
  ((OR (EQL A 121) (EQL A 89)) (CONCLUDE (ASCII A)))
  ((OR (EQL A 110) (EQL A 78)) (PRINC (ASCII A))))
 (TONE 30000 2000) (MAKE-WINDOW 0 0 25 80) (CLEAR-SCREEN))

(DEFUN VERIFY (FACT RULE FACT-RULES IF-PARTS SPOK TEMP-
RULES)
 ((MEMBER FACT FACTS 'EQUAL) (RETURN T))
```

```
 (SETQ FACT-RULES (COLLECT-RULES FACT RULES))
 (SETQ EXIT 'EXIT)
 (COND ((AND (NULL FACT-RULES) (NOT (MEMBER FACT ASKED
'EQUAL)))
     (SETQ EXIT (ASK-THE-USER FACT RULE))))
 ((EQL EXIT NIL) (RETURN NIL))
 ((EQL EXIT T) (RETURN T))
 ((AND (NULL FACT-RULES) (MEMBER FACT ASKED 'EQUAL))
(RETURN NIL))
 (SETQ SPOK NIL)
 (SETQ TEMP-RULES FACT-RULES)
 (LOOP
  ((NULL TEMP-RULES))
  (SETQ SPOK (TRYRULE1 (CAR TEMP-RULES)))
  ((EQL SPOK T))
  (SETQ TEMP-RULES (CDR TEMP-RULES)))
 ((EQL SPOK T) (RETURN T))
 (LOOP
  ((NULL FACT-RULES))
  (SETQ SPOK (TRYRULE2 (CAR FACT-RULES) FACT-RULES))
  ((EQL SPOK T))
  (SETQ FACT-RULES (CDR FACT-RULES)))
 (COND ((EQL SPOK T) (RETURN T))
    ((EQL SPOK NIL) (RETURN NIL))))

(DEFUN TRYRULE2 (RULE FACT-RULES TWO TCON THEN-PARTS
IF-PART)
 (SETQ THEN-PARTS (GET-THEN-PART RULE))
 (SETQ TWO T)
 (LOOP
  ((NULL THEN-PARTS))
  (SETQ TCON (FIND-CONFLICTS (CAR THEN-PARTS) CONFLICTS))
  (LOOP
   ((NULL TCON))
   ((MEMBER (CAR TCON) FACTS 'EQUAL) (RETURN NIL))
   (SETQ TCON (CDR TCON)))
  (SETQ THEN-PARTS (CDR THEN-PARTS)))
 (SETQ IF-PARTS (GET-IF-PART RULE))
 (LOOP
```

```
  ((NULL IF-PARTS))
  (SETQ TWO (VERIFY (CAR IF-PARTS) RULE FACT-RULES IF-
PARTS))
  ((EQL TWO NIL) (RETURN NIL))
  (SETQ IF-PARTS (CDR IF-PARTS)))
 (COND
  ((EQL TWO T) (ADD-THEN-PARTS 'FACTS RULE)
   (MAKE-WINDOW 1 52 23 27) (CLEAR-SCREEN) (PRINC "
FACTS")
   (TERPRI) (PRINC "        -----") (HELP-PRINT FACTS)
   (SETQ UP-TO-NOW (EXPAND-LIST (GET-THEN-PART RULE) UP-
TO-NOW)) (RETURN T))))
```

Bibliography

Argyle, M - "Social Interaction". Tavistock, London, 1973.

Austin, J L - "How to do things with words" - The William James Lectures delivered at Harvard University in 1955. Ed. J O Urmson. Oxford University Press, 1982.

Barr, A & Feigenbaum, E A - "The Handbook of Artificial Intelligence". Vol 1. Pitman, 1983.

Bliss, J & Ogborn, J - "The analysis of qualitative data". European Journal of Science Education. 1,4, 1979.

Bonnet, A - "A.I. Promise and preformance". Prentice Hall, 1985.

Brooks, F P - "The mythical man month - Essays on software engineering". Addison Wesley, 1982.

Brownston, L, Farrell, R, Kant, E & Martin, N - "Programming Expert Systems in OPS5". Addison Wesley, 1985.

Bryant, N - "Managing Expert Systems". John Wiley & sons, 1988.

Cannel, C F & Kahn, R L - "Interviewing". In Lindsey & Aronson (eds) "Handbook of Social Psychology" Vol 2, 2nd edn. Addison Wesley, 1968.

Charniak, E & McDermott, D - "Introduction to Artificial Intelligence". Addison Wesley, 1985.

Davis, R - "Interactive Transfer of Expertise". Originally in Artificial Intelligence 12, 121-157, 1979. Shortened version now in Buchanan & Shortliffe, "Rule Based Expert Systems" - Addison Wesley, 1984.

Doukidis, G I & Paul, R J - "ASPES: A Skeletal Pascal Expert System" in: Sol, H G et al. (eds) "Expert Systems and Artificial Intelligence in Decision Support Systems". Reidel Publishing Company, The Netherlands, 1987.

Doukidis, G I, Shah, V P & Angelides, M C - "LISP : from foundations to applications". Chartwell - Bratt, 1988.

Doukidis, G I & Whitley, E A - "Developing and running Expert Systems with PESYS". "Future Generation Computer Systems", North Holland Publishing, forthcoming Summer 1988.

Dreyfus, H L & Dreyfus, S E - "Mind over machine". Blackwell, 1986.

Feigenbaum, E A - "Knowledge Engineering for the 1980's". Department of Computer Science, Standford University, Stanford California, 1982.

Fickas, S - "Supporting the programmer of a rule based language". Expert Systems Vol 4, No 2, Page 73. 1987.

Flanagan, J C - "The critical incident technique". Psychological bulletin, 1954.

Gammack, J G & Young, R M - "A pragmatic knowledge acquisition methodology". Proceedings of IJCAI-8, 1985.

Harmon, P & King, D - "Expert Systems, Artificial Intelligence in Business". John Wiley, 1986.

Harmon, P & Maus, R & Morrissey W - "Expert Systems, Tools and Applications". John Wiley, 1988.

Hart, A - "Knowledge acquisition for Expert Systems". Kogan Page, 1986.

Hayes, R S - "Developing a Protocol-Based Expert Model of the Decision Process of International Bank Credit Officers" in Doukidis, G I, Land, F & Miller, G (Eds) "Knowledge based Management Support Systems", Ellis Horwood, forthcoming 1988.

Humphreys, P - "Levels of Representation in structuring decision problems". Journal of Applied Systems Analysis, Vol 11, 1984.

Humphreys, P - "Intelligence in decision support - A process model". in Doukidis, G I, Land, F & Miller, G (Eds) "Knowledge based Management Support Systems", Ellis Horwood, forthcoming 1988.

Ives, B & Learmonth, G P - "The information system as a competitive weapon", Communications of the ACM, Vol 27, No 12, December 1984.

Jackson, P - "Introduction to Expert Systems". Addison-Wesley, 1986.

Kapila & Nagpal - "Designing and validating an Expert System - A cricketing analogy". Internal Research Paper, SAIDS Group, Department of Information Systems. London School of Economics and Political Science, 1988.

Keller, R - "Expert System Technology". Yourdon Press, Prentice Hall, 1987.

Kelly, G A - "The psychology of personal constructs". Norton, New York, 1955.

Krech, D - "Theory and problems of social psychology. McGraw Hill, 1948.

Kuhn, T S - "The structure of scientific revolution". University of Chicago Press, 1962.

Land, F, Cornford, T & Doukidis, G I - "In search of the Expert System Product ". Expert Systems for Information Management, forthcoming, Autumn, 1988.

Minsky, M - "Matter, Mind and Models" in "Semantic Information Processing". MIT Press, 1968.

Moore, K M - "Delivering Expert Systems in practice". Institution of Electrical Engineers, Computing and Control Division, Professional group C4, on "Testing Expert Systems". Digest No. 1987/110. December 3rd, 1987.

Newell, A & Simon, H A - "Human Problem Solving". Prentice Hall, 1972.

O'Keefe, R M, Balci, O, Smith, E P - "Validating Expert System Performance". IEEE Expert, Winter 1987.

Poulymenakou, A & Doukidis, G I - "A knowledge acquisition case study: towards an intergrated approach of knowledge elicitation techniques". Internal Research Paper, SAIDS Group, Department of Information Systems. London School of Economics and Political Science, 1987.

Poulymenakou, A & Doukidis, G I - "Towards an integrated approach of knowledge acquisition" to be submitted to the "Expert Systems 88", 1988 conference of the British Computer Society Special Interest Group in Expert Systems, Brighton, December 1988.

Rich, E - "Artificial Intelligence". McGraw Hill, 1983.

Searle, J R - "Speech Acts" . Cambridge University Press, 1969.

Searle, J R - "The philosophy of language", Oxford University Press, 1971.

Sell, P - "Expert Systems - A practical introduction". Camelot press, 1985.

Shaw, M L G - "Recent advances in personal construct technology". Academic Press, New York. 1981.

Shirai, Y & Tsujii,J - "Artificial Intelligence: Concepts, Techniques and Applications". John Wiley, 1984.

Shortliffe, E - "Rule-based expert systems: The MYCIN experiments of the Standford Heuristics Programming Project". Addison-Wesley, 1984.

Stamper, R K & Backhouse, J & Marche, S & Althaus, K - "Semantic Normal Form?". Proceeding Aslib Conference, Informatics 9, Meaning : the Frontier of Informatics, 1987.

Stamper, R K -"Pathologies of AI: Responsible use of Artificial Intelligence in Professional Work". AI & Society, Vol 2, 1988.

Turing, A M - "Computing machinery and intelligence". Mind Vol LIX, No 236, 1950. Reprinted in "Minds & Machines", Ed. Anderson, A R. Prentice Hall, 1964.

Waterman, D & Jenkins, B - "Heuristic modeling using rule-based computer systems". In Kupperman, R & Trent, D (eds) "Terrorism, Threat, Reality, Response: Selected readings". Hooner Institute Press, Stanford University, California, 1979.

Weiss, S M & Kulikowski, C A - "A practical guide to designing Expert Systems". Rowman & Allenheld, 1984.

Welbank, M - "A review of Knowledge Acquisition Techniques for Expert Systems". British Telecom Research Laboratories, Martlesham Heath, Ipswich, 1983.

Wicks, R P - "Interviewing". In Cooper, C L & Makin, P "Psychology for managers". British Psychological Society & Macmillan Publishers, 1984.

Wielinga, B J & Breuker, J A - "Interpretation of verbal data for knowledge acquisition". In O'Shea (ed) "Advances in artificial Intelligence". North Holland, 1984.

Winograd, T & Flores F - "Understanding Computers and Cognition". Ablex Publishing Corporation, 1986.

Winston, P H - "Aritificial Intelligence". Addison Wesley, 1984.

Winston, P H & Horn, B K P - "Lisp", second edition. Addison-Wesley, 1984.

Wisden - "Wisden Cricketers' Almanack 1983 (120th year)". Macdonald & co. Ltd. for John Wisden & Co. Ltd., 1983.

Index

Compiled by Indexing Specialists, 202 Church Road, Hove, East Sussex, BN3 2DJ, United Kingdom.

Computing Books from Chartwell-Bratt

GENERAL COMPUTING BOOKS

Compiler Physiology for Beginners, M Farmer, 279pp, ISBN 0-86238-064-2
Dictionary of Computer and Information Technology, D Lynch, 225 pages, ISBN 0-86238-128-2
File Structure and Design, M Cunningham, 211pp, ISBN 0-86238-065-0
Information Technology Dictionary of Acronyms and Abbreviations, D Lynch, 270pp, ISBN 0-86238-153-3
The IBM Personal Computer with BASIC and PC-DOS, B Kynning, 320pp, ISBN 0-86238-080-4

PROGRAMMING LANGUAGES

An Intro to LISP, P Smith, 130pp, ISBN 0-86238-187-8
An Intro to OCCAM 2 Programming, Bowler, *et al,* 109pp, ISBN 0-86238-137-1
Cobol for Mainframe and Micro, D Watson, 177pp, ISBN 0-86238-082-0
Comparative Languages: 2nd Ed, J R Malone, 125pp, ISBN 0-86238-123-1
First Ada, P Woolliams & J Peacham, 180pp, ISBN 0-86238-116-9
Fortran 77 for Non-Scientists, P Adman, 109pp, ISBN 0-86238-074-X
Fortran 77 Solutions to Non-Scientific Problems, P Adman, 150pp, ISBN 0-86238-087-1
Fortran Lectures at Oxford, F Pettit, 135pp, ISBN 0-86238-122-3
LISP: From Foundations to Applications, G Doukidis *et al,* 228pp, ISBN 0-86238-191-6
Programming Language Semantics, C Rattray, 135pp, ISBN 0-86238-066-9
Simula Begin, G M Birtwistle *et al,* 391pp, ISBN 0-86238-009-X
The Intensive C Course, M Farmer, 167pp, ISBN 0-86238-114-2
The Intensive Pascal Course, M Farmer, 111pp, ISBN 0-86238-063-4

ASSEMBLY LANGUAGE PROGRAMMING

Coding the 68000, N Hellawell, 214pp, ISBN 0-86238-180-0
Computer Organisation and Assembly Language Programming, L Ohlsson & P Stenstrom, 128pp, ISBN 0-86238-129-0
What is machine code and what can you do with it? N Hellawell, 104pp, ISBN 0-86238-132-0

PROGRAMMING TECHNIQUES

Discrete-events simulations models in PASCAL/MT+ on a microcomputer, L P Jennergren, 135pp, ISBN 0-86238-053-7
Information and Coding, J A Llewellyn, 152pp, ISBN 0-86238-099-5
JSP - A Practical Method of Program Design, L Ingevaldsson, 204pp, ISBN 0-86238-107-X

JSD - Method for System Development, L Ingevaldsson, 248pp,
ISBN 0-86238-103-7
Linear Programming: A Computational Approach: 2nd Ed, K K Lau, 150pp,
ISBN 0-86238-182-7

Programming for Beginners: the structured way, D Bell & P Scott, 178pp,
ISBN 0-86238-130-4
Software Engineering for Students, M Coleman & S Pratt, 195pp,
ISBN 0-86238-115-0
Software Taming with Dimensional Design, M Coleman & S Pratt, 164pp,
ISBN 0-86238-142-8
Systems Programming with JSP, B Sanden, 186pp, ISBN 0-86238-054-5

MATHEMATICS AND COMPUTING

Fourier Transforms in Action, F Pettit, 133pp, ISBN 0-86238-088-X
Generalised Coordinates, L G Chambers, 90pp, ISBN 0-86238-079-0
Statistics and Operations Research, I P Schagen, 300pp,
ISBN 0-86238-077-4
Teaching of Modern Engineering Mathematics, L Rade (ed), 225pp,
ISBN 0-86238-173-8
Teaching of Statistics in the Computer Age, L Rade (ed), 248pp,
ISBN 0-86238-090-1
The Essentials of Numerical Computation, M Bartholomew-Biggs, 241pp,
ISBN 0-86238-029-4

DATABASES AND MODELLING

Database Analysis and Design, H Robinson, 378pp, ISBN 0-86238-018-9
Databases and Database Systems, E Oxborrow, 256pp, ISBN 0-86238-091-X
Data Bases and Data Models, B Sundgren, 134pp, ISBN 0-86238-031-6
Towards Transparent Databases, G Sandstrom, 192pp, ISBN 0-86238-095-2
Information Modelling, J Bubenko (ed), 687pp, ISBN 0-86238-006-5

UNIX

An Intro to the Unix Operating System, C Duffy, 152pp,
ISBN 0-86238-143-6
Operating Systems through Unix, G Emery, 96pp, ISBN 0-86238-086-3

SYSTEMS ANALYSIS AND DEVELOPMENT

Systems Analysis and Development: 2nd Ed, P Layzell & P Loucopoulos, 232pp,
ISBN 0-86238-156-8

SYSTEMS DESIGN

Computer Systems: Where Hardware meets Software, C Machin, 200pp, ISBN 0-86238-075-8

Distributed Applications and Online Dialogues: a design method for application systems, A Rasmussen, 271pp, ISBN 0-86238-105-3

HARDWARE

Computers from First Principles, M Brown, 128pp, ISBN 0-86238-027-8
Fundamentals of Microprocessor Systems, P Witting, 525pp, ISBN 0-86238-030-8

NETWORKS

Communication Network Protocols: 2nd Ed, B Marsden, 345pp, ISBN 0-86238-106-1
Computer Networks: Fundamentals and Practice, M D Bacon *et al,* 109pp, ISBN 0-86238-028-6
Datacommunication: Data Networks, Protocols and Design, L Ewald & E Westman, 350pp, ISBN 0-86238-092-8
Telecommunications: Telephone Networks 1, Ericsson & Televerket, 147pp, ISBN 0-86238-093-6
Telecommunications: Telephone Networks 2, Ericsson & Televerket, 176pp, ISBN 0-86238-113-4

GRAPHICS

An Introductory Course in Computer Graphics, R Kingslake, 146pp, ISBN 0-86238-073-1
Techniques of Interactive Computer Graphics, A Boyd, 242pp, ISBN 0-86238-024-3
Two-dimensional Computer Graphics, S Laflin, 85pp, ISBN 0-86238-127-4

APPLICATIONS

Computers in Health and Fitness, J Abas, 106pp, ISBN 0-86238-155-X
Developing Expert Systems, G Doukidis, E Whitley, ISBN 0-86238-196-7
Expert Systems Introduced, D Daly, 180pp, ISBN 0-86238-185-1
Handbook of Finite Element Software, J Mackerle & B Fredriksson, approx 1000pp, ISBN 0-86238-135-5
Inside Data Processing: computers and their effective use in business, A deWatteville, 150pp, ISBN 0-86238-181-9
Proceedings of the Third Scandinavian Conference on Image Analysis, P Johansen & P Becker (eds) 426pp, ISBN 0-86238-039-1
Programmable Control Systems, G Johannesson, 136pp, ISBN 0-86238-046-4
Risk and Reliability Appraisal on Microcomputers, G Singh, with G Kiangi, 142pp, ISBN 0-86238-159-2
Statistics with Lotus 1-2-3, M Lee & J Soper, 207pp, ISBN 0-86238-131-2

HCI

Human/Computer Interaction: from voltage to knowledge, J Kirakowski, 250pp, ISBN 0-86238-179-7
Information Ergonomics, T Ivegard, 228pp, ISBN 0-86238-032-4
Computer Display Designer's Handbook, E Wagner, approx 300pp, ISBN 0-86238-171-1

INFORMATION AND SOCIETY

Access to Government Records: International Perspectives and Trends, T Riley, 112pp, ISBN 0-86238-119-3
CAL/CBT - the great debate, D Marshall, 300pp, ISBN 0-86238-144-4
Economic and Trade-Related Aspects of Transborder Dataflow, R Wellington-Brown, 93pp, ISBN 0-86238-110-X
Information Technology and a New International Order, J Becker, 141pp, ISBN 0-86238-043-X
Three Perspectives on Information Systems, M Nurminen, 1218pp, ISBN 0-86238-184-3
Transnational Data Flows in the Information Age, C Hamelink, 115pp, ISBN 0-86238-042-1

SCIENCE HANDBOOKS

Alpha Maths Handbook, L Rade, 199pp, ISBN 0-86238-036-7
Beta Maths Handbook, L Rade, 425pp, ISBN 0-86238-140-1
Handbook of Electronics, J de Sousa Pires, approx 750pp, ISBN 0-86238-061-8
Nuclear Analytical Chemistry, D Brune *et al,* 557pp, ISBN 0-86238-047-2
Physics Handbook, C Nordling & J Osterman, 430pp, ISBN 0-86238-037-5
The V-Belt Handbook, H Palmgren, 287pp, ISBN 0-86238-111-8

Chartwell-Bratt specialise in excellent books at affordable prices.

For further details contact your local bookshop, or ring Chartwell-Bratt direct on **01-467 1956** (Access/Visa welcome.)

Ring or write for our *free* catalogue.

Chartwell-Bratt (Publishing & Training) Ltd, Old Orchard, Bickley Road, Bromley, Kent, BR1 2NE, United Kingdom.
Tel 01-467 1956, Fax 01-467 1754, Telecom Gold 84:KJM001,
Telex 9312100451(CB)

An Introduction to LISP

by Peter Smith

This readable introduction to a difficult programming language is aimed chiefly at undergraduates of computer science and other disciplines, although its *clarity of approach* - featuring a minimum of technical jargon - will commend it to anyone who wishes to learn LISP, without having studied another language.

A special feature of the book is the *optional sections for those whose first language is Pascal.* Comparisons between LISP and Pascal are made, which readers with no Pascal knowledge can safely omit without jeopardising their understanding of LISP.

The reader is progressively introduced to the **concepts, structure, functions, and operations of LISP,** with later chapters covering more *advanced* material. Three chapters concentrate on the use of LISP within *Artificial Intelligence* - including a **complete working expert system** which is explained in detail. Hints on writing better LISP programs are given where appropriate. **End of chapter summaries and exercises with solutions are a valuable feature.**

Contents: *Introduction: what is LISP? A look at LISP proper; More on functions; List processing operations; Making choices in LISP; Repetitive operations in LISP; More list processing functions; Further recursion; Advanced list operations; Various LISP functions; Applications of LISP - knowledge structures; Applications of LISP - natural language processing; An introduction to the theory of LISP; Answers to exercises*

1988, 130 pages, ISBN 0-86238-187-8 ***Low Price !!***

For current price details, contact your local bookshop or Chartwell-Bratt direct. **Chartwell-Bratt**, Old Orchard, Bickley Road, Bromley, Kent, United Kingdom, BR1 2NE, Tel 01-467 1956, Fax 01-467 1754